Sentimental
Savannah

Sentimental

Savannah

Reflections on a Southern City's Past

Polly Powers Stramm

Charleston   London

History
PRESS

Published by The History Press
Charleston, SC 29403
www.historypress.net

Front cover: In the 1930s Elizabeth Pierce, Pauline Cargill and Margaret Egloff modeled for a brochure promoting sports at Tybee Island. *Courtesy of the author.*

First published 2006

Manufactured in the United Kingdom

ISBN 1.59629.140.0

Library of Congress Cataloging-in-Publication Data

Stramm, Polly Powers, 1954-
Sentimental Savannah : reflections on a southern city's past / Polly Powers Stramm.
p. cm.
ISBN 1-59629-140-0 (alk. paper)
1. Savannah (Ga.)--Social life and customs--20th century--Anecdotes. 2.
Savannah (Ga.)--Biography--Anecdotes. 3. Savannah (Ga.)--History--20th
century--Anecdotes. I. Title.
F294.S2S76 2006
975.8'724043--dc22
                        2006020413

Notice: The information in this book is true and complete to the best of our knowledge. It is offered without guarantee on the part of the author or The History Press. The author and The History Press disclaim all liability in connection with the use of this book.

Contents

Introduction

In 1987 I asked Wallace M. Davis Jr., who was then executive editor of the *Savannah Morning News* and *Evening Press*, if I could write a weekly column about people. At first I thought it could be called "Polly's People and Places." But knowing Wally, he probably said something like, "Golly Polly, I think it should be called 'Polly's People.'"

Today, nearly one thousand columns later, which ran both in the *Evening Press* and the *Morning News*, I'm still writing about people (and places, too). I've selected pieces for this book that relate to Savannah's magical connection to the past—physically, as when seeing the cityscape of two hundred-year-old homes and buildings through the curtains of Spanish moss dripping from ancient oaks, and emotionally, through residents who recall their Savannah, the way it was and the way it is now.

I've included memories of Tybee Island, Daffin Park and the people and places in between, like Arthur Brannen, the premier Savannah character who wore white boots and carried white buckets while riding his bicycle. I've condensed a few and improved on others. As a colleague told me once: "You write and rewrite until you get it right."

My own journalism journey began years ago when I rode a bicycle to Charles Ellis School and wrote about "The View From My Window" in Mary Price's sixth-grade class. Later, I was news editor of the *Blue and White* at Savannah High School and became a journalism major at the University of Georgia.

When I was living in a UGA dormitory, my parents gave me a subscription to what was then a new magazine, called *People Weekly*. This was long before cell phones and e-mail, so finding both mail and magazines in the dormitory mailbox definitely brightened my day.

I had fallen in love with *People* the day I spotted the first issue, the one with Mia Farrow as *The Great Gatsby*'s Daisy Buchanan on the cover. Every Tuesday, after I unlocked my mailbox and grabbed the magazine, I would return to my room and read it from cover to cover. Back then, I never skimmed it; I read each story, word for word, before turning the page to the next one.

While I was at UGA I wrote for the student newspaper, the *Red and Black*. One of my stories was a first-person account of attending President Jimmy Carter's inauguration. It's a shame that I don't remember what Carter said because I was more interested in the tiniest of details, like what Rosalynn Carter and others wore to the inaugural balls.

This was back in the investigative reporting days of Bob Woodward and Carl Bernstein. Every journalism major, it seems, wanted to be like them. Me? I wasn't so sure. I ended up covering fires, murders and other big stories during my years as a reporter for the *Savannah Morning News* and *Evening Press*, but people stories quickly became my forte. In fact, it was my first editor at the newspaper, Martha Giddens Nesbit, who in 1978 advised me to find what I do best and write those kinds of stories. Eventually, I did.

Oh, did I mention that for the last couple of years I have been a stringer for *People* magazine's Miami bureau? What more could a girl want?

Old Savannah postcard. *Courtesy of the author.*

Acknowledgements

I couldn't have done this book without the support of the *Savannah Morning News*, in particular Publisher Julian Miller and Executive Editor Susan Catron, who publish my column on a weekly basis. I also appreciate the opportunity given to me by others who came before them at "the paper"—especially Wallace M. Davis Jr., Kathy Haeberle and Tom Coffey, who never lets me forget the letter to the editor I wrote to him when I was a student at the University of Georgia. Going way back, I am indebted to Martha Giddens Nesbit, who hired me at the paper when I was a polliwog just out of journalism school.

As always, I appreciate the hard work and guidance of *Morning News* Chief Photographer Steve Bisson and Research Librarians Julia Muller and Sara Wright. My good friend, author Kathy Hogan Trocheck, who also writes

Pledge to the flag. *Courtesy of the* Savannah Morning News.

under the name Mary Kay Andrews, is always there as a sounding board with excellent advice and suggestions.

I am extremely grateful to The History Press for asking me to do a book of columns that I've written during the last twenty years. I thank them for giving me both the incentive and the deadlines.

Last but not least I owe everything to my family—my husband, Steve, my daughters, Polly and Mary, and my parents, Lee and Pauline Powers—as well as the people who have shared their precious memories with me.

Part I

Unforgettable Characters

Years After His "Pop" Went Broke, Lyricist Johnny Mercer Paid His Debts

It's a story akin to the classic tearjerker *It's a Wonderful Life.* But this time it's fact, not a fictional movie, and it's about a son—actually a native son named Johnny Mercer—who made good on his father's financial troubles.

I had heard bits and pieces of the story before, how after becoming rich and famous, Mercer paid his father's debts, keeping a promise he made years before. Now Mercer family friend Nick Mamalakis has detailed the facts for me.

"Johnny swore to his brother Walter to keep it secret," Mamalakis wrote. "I knew the story was too big and we couldn't keep the cap on the bottle." His brother refused to talk but somehow the story got out and "all hell broke loose in New York and Los Angeles."

Here's how Mamalakis remembers the story with the happy ending:

In 1927, Johnny Mercer came home for spring break from Woodberry Forest Prep School just as the nation's financial roof fell in and panic engulfed America. Johnny's father was a successful real estate man whose business, the G.A. Mercer Company, managed properties, handled sales and issued saving certificates.

"People began making runs on the banks, withdrawing their savings, and forcing the banks into bankruptcy," Mamalakis wrote. "The Mercer Company experienced the same run on its certificates. Because its funds were invested in sound real estate properties, Mr. Mercer chose to put the company into court under an orderly liquidation plan."

On the date set for document signing, Johnny Mercer was in his "Pop's" office asking for movie tickets. Mr. Mercer asked Johnny to come to the signing. Johnny overheard the conversation between his father and George W. Hunt, president of Chatham Savings Bank, which was the selected liquidation agent. Johnny asked Hunt how much money would be needed to avoid the planned auction.

"Can you raise me a quick $1.5 million, Johnny?" Hunt asked. Johnny said, "Not today, Mr. Hunt, but some day, if I make it big I'll see that anyone who bet on my father will not lose a dime."

Lyricist Johnny "Moon River" Mercer never forgot his hometown. *Courtesy of the* Savannah Morning News.

Johnny's father went broke, and Johnny withdrew from school.

The years rolled by, and true to G.A. Mercer's predictions, real estate rebounded, Mamalakis said.

Meanwhile, Johnny Mercer's music and songwriting career prospered, and during the next three decades he became one of America's greatest lyricists. He and several friends founded Capitol Records, which he later sold for "a ton," Mamalakis wrote.

One day Walter Mercer, who by then was president of Mercer Insurance Agency, was sitting with Mamalakis, his vice-president, with whom he had an "almost father-son relationship."

"Suddenly there was a knock on the back door," Mamalakis recalled. It was George Hunt, who told Walter Mercer that after all these years he had gotten a letter from Johnny, who wrote it while riding a train between New York and Los Angeles and dropped it off in Chicago. He asked Hunt for the balance due on the certificates of his father's old company.

Hunt told the two men that Johnny had no obligation for this debt and asked what he should do. Walter Mercer's reply? "Give him the information."

Three weeks later there was another knock on the back door. It was Hunt again. "That crazy Johnny mailed me a check, but he forgot to sign it."

After Hunt left, Mercer and Mamalakis discussed an idea raised by Mamalakis, who knew of Johnny's endearing love for his parents. Mamalakis thought Johnny should use the money to establish college scholarships in his parents' names.

Walter Mercer asked Mamalakis to write Johnny and tell him about the scholarship idea. He also enclosed the unsigned check for Johnny to sign. Shortly afterward, Mamalakis heard back from Johnny. He sent the signed $300,000 check and Mamalakis's letter about the scholarship idea. He wrote on the bottom: "Nick, you are talking with your head and I'm speaking with my heart!" He signed it with a big "J."

After paying off certificate holders and deducting final expenses, Chatham Bank sent Johnny $45,000 from the sale of the last real estate parcel. Johnny divided it three ways: the Episcopal Church the Elks Hospital for Children in Atlanta and the Jenkins Boys' Club in Savannah, which named its new gym in honor of Johnny's father.

First published in 2001 in the Savannah Morning News.

Seymour Kandel Reminisces About Savannah, Family Life and the Tybee Train

As a child, Seymour Kandel remembers folks running to catch the Tybee train so they could sit on the train's red velvet seats.

"If we got the red velvet seats we were in high cotton," said eighty-five-year-old Seymour, who recalls spending time at Tybee like it was yesterday. His family's association with the beach began in the early 1900s when Seymour's father, who was a hat man and operated Kandel the Hatter on Broughton Street, built two duplexes on the Strand at Tybee. The structures were built on the site of what was to become the Solms Hotel and, currently, condominiums.

"Daddy liked to play cards," Seymour recalled. "It was written in stone that every Saturday night the women would keep the coffeepot going and bake, and the men would play cards."

Although he was only a little tyke when his family stayed at Tybee, Seymour has vivid memories of life at the beach. He often hung around with regular fishermen who spread out their nets on the beach. He tagged along with the fishermen when they went house to house selling their catch.

"Henry Buckley was the head lifeguard and my brother would help him," he said. "There was the Brass Rail, the Hotel Tybee and another place called the Durden and Powers Bathhouse. Mr. Powers ran the bathhouse for the Central of Georgia Railroad."

The train made different stops on certain days, he said. Some days it would stop at Boyd's Fishing Camp. Next it would stop at Byers's place and then Fort Screven to bring the mail and ice. "It would stop right at the parade grounds, which were beautiful," he said.

After the turn there was Smith's Store, Lovell Station, Dixon Station and Mr. May the iceman. Stopping at the Hotel Tybee was a grand experience. The hotel had a long porte cache and big luggage wagons like the ones at Savannah's Union Station, Seymour said.

The turntable was near a big tank at Venetian Terrace. Workers would turn the engine around and flip the red velvet and straw seats.

The Tybee train was in operation from the late 1800s until the early 1930s. *Courtesy of the author.*

The Kandels kept their Tybee place until the 1920s, when Seymour's father died.

Seymour's father came to America from Austria at age twelve. He ended up out West where he worked for "Mr. Stetson, the cowboy hat man."

"Men drank out of those hats, washed themselves and fed their horses out of those hats," Seymour said.

One day, Seymour's father told Stetson he wasn't making any money selling the big cowboy hats but he had an idea for a smaller hat. Stetson thought it was a good idea and sent Seymour's father to Washington.

In a few years he moved to Baltimore, made a pushcart and began selling his hats on the street. He lived next door to a man who owned a beer and soft drink company and ended up also selling soft drinks, as well as hats, on his cart. During those years the enterprising young man made enough money to bring two of his brothers over from Austria.

Eventually, Seymour's father worked his way down the eastern seaboard and arrived at Savannah's Union Station in the pouring rain. "It was raining so hard he couldn't get across West Broad Street. He had to pay a man a dollar to take him across the street in a wagon."

After his father died, the family and the country fell on hard times, Seymour said.

"Harvey Granger was the manager of the Penn Mutual Life Insurance Co.," Seymour said. "My mother went to him and said she would like a job selling insurance." At first, Granger hesitated because there was no such thing as a female in insurance, Seymour said. He then gave Mrs. Kandel a chance and she worked for the company for forty-two years.

Seymour had two older brothers, one of whom was Dr. Harry Kandel, a well-known college football player. Seymour himself attended Benedictine Military School on an athletic scholarship.

During those years, the Kandels' Savannah address was 505 West 36th Street. Eventually a family with an attractive daughter named Helen moved just behind them. Seymour had known Helen before but got to know her even better when they became neighbors.

"The best money I ever spent was for a marriage license," he recalled.

First published in 2001 in the Morning News.

I "Loved Ya," Bill,
How Could I Resist?

Every November 27 since 1982 I've received a telephone call from my dear friend Bill Canty. Always when I picked up the phone I knew right away who was on the other end.

The conversations always went something like this: "Polly dahlin'," he would say in his old Savannah accent, "I want to wish you a happy anniversary. I'll never forget your wedding." His brief calls were sprinkled with words like "wonderful" and "grand" and, always, he would tell me how much he loved me.

The same was true with the cards he sent. He usually included a sweet note in his steady, flowing handwriting and his trademark, "Love ya, Bill."

Sadly those phone calls and notes won't come anymore, because my buddy Bill died two weeks ago today.

I'm grateful that I met that sweet little Irishman all those years ago in the Catholic Cemetery. I had heard about an eighty-year-old man whose hobby was to clean tombstones, and I thought his story would interest readers.

Thus began a friendship that would last for nearly twenty years. But oh how I wish I had known him longer. Bill brought such joy to my life.

That day in the cemetery he told me how he cleaned the stones of people who didn't have heirs. He was proud of his own lot, marked Canty-Brennan-Nesbitt, which already had a stone with his name inscribed.

"I'm going here," he said, laughing. "Mama will have us all around to talk to."

I soon learned that it was not uncommon for Bill to talk about death, but certainly not in a morbid fashion. I suppose that was part of his Irish upbringing.

When we met, Bill was living in an apartment at Lester Hayman Funeral Home on Victory Drive. He had moved there after selling his family's Henry Street home. Every morning he walked across the street to Mass at Blessed Sacrament.

Bill Canty cleaned tombstones in the Catholic Cemetery as a hobby. *Courtesy of the* Savannah Morning News.

At that time, he was delighted to find out that I was engaged. (Bill never married but told me several years later that when he was young he had fallen in love with a girl who became a nun. A few years ago he visited her grave at Belmont Abbey.)

Bill sent a wedding gift and arranged for the funeral home's limousine to pick us up at the church and take us to the reception. I had just turned twenty-eight when I took my first limo ride that November evening.

Our friendship flourished. Through the years he called and sent cards and I tried to do the same. Somehow—in what I would say is an only-in-Savannah moment—I discovered that we had a mutual friend in Bunnie Richey, whose late father had worked with Bill. For the last several years Bunnie and I would take Bill to lunch at Johnny Harris's Restaurant to celebrate his birthday and Christmas.

He would regale us with stories of growing up with his "Mama and Papa" and how he still felt like he was sixteen. He had a tremendously positive outlook and would often poke fun at himself, saying he was an "old man with one eye, no hair and no teeth."

He was such a charmer.

Eventually Bill went to live at Rose of Sharon Apartments. Last November when Bunnie and I took him to lunch he was not as spry as he had been. Mentally he was as sharp as ever, but he was depending on a walker more and more. But, after all, he was almost ninety-eight then and he had just buried the last of nine siblings.

Just days later Bill went to sit down, hit the arm of the chair and plopped down on the floor, hurting his back. He was hardly the same afterward.

I remember the last time Bunnie and I took him to lunch. Naturally the topic of conversation once again turned to death (if you were around Bill, it had to!). He told us that when his time came he wanted a brief graveside service because he didn't want to trouble anyone.

His wish came true on a rainy Thursday morning. At first I wanted to curse the heavens for the downpour that occurred during Bill's funeral. After all, even Bishop Kevin Boland came to bid him farewell.

But after thinking about my sweet friend and his connections upstairs, I decided those weren't chilly raindrops at all. The angels were crying tears of joy because dear Bill had finally joined the chorus.

First published in 2002 in the Morning News.

Remer Lane Follows Through with Father's Love of History

It's difficult for Remer Lane Jr. to take credit for a charming little book he published.

"I didn't do a thing," he insists. "My father was always interested in local history and, when he retired, he recorded a session with Mr. Louie Mathews, who was the dean of wholesale and retail fishing in Savannah."

The interview is the subject of the book called simply *A Conversation With Louis C. Mathews*, conducted by Remer Y. Lane and transcribed and edited by Remer Y. Lane Jr. Remer published the book with the help of graphic artist Gene Carpenter.

"Gene literally did all the work," Remer said. "If anything, I guess I was the catalyst. It's a tribute to my father and Mr. Mathews, and something my father wanted done."

The conversation took place at Mathews Seafood on West Broad Street during December 1976. The book is filled with interesting fish tales and other tidbits, such as how Mathews's Italian name was changed:

> *I'm going to tell you how my daddy got the name Mathews. Years back right after he got married he went to the C&S Bank and talked to Mr. Gleason and opened an account. He gave them his Italian bankbook. The Italian bankbook read: "Cannarella Metteo"—the Italians always put the last name first. So Mr. Gleason put down "C. Mathews." That's how come his name came to be Mathews. Really and truly—that's the genuine truth.*

The Mathews's tapes were "languishing in my father's library," Remer said, until Remer's mother, Louise, went through some things and asked her son to "take care" of them.

Remer's father "abhorred the spotlight" but he loved history. He often taped conversations with people he thought were important to the local landscape, whether it was Savannah where other subjects included fishermen Gilbert Maggioni and James Adams, or the South Carolina Lowcountry, which the Lanes once called home.

Remer Lane Sr. was one of the founders of Johnson, Lane & Space (stockbrokers) but decided he wanted to be a farmer instead of a stockbroker, his son said.

"In 1945 he bought a place in South Carolina where we lived until we came to Savannah," Remer said. He also has tapes his father recorded of South Carolinians speaking Gullah, a kind of Creole blend of English and African languages.

"This is the kind of thing that needs to be preserved," Remer said. "When something like Gullah dies, it's gone forever."

Remer kept a few books, gave several to the Mathews family and will sell the rest to create what he describes as a revolving fund for similar volumes.

First published in 2001 in the Morning News.

Mildred Gartelmann's Life:
A Tapestry of the Century

When Mildred Gartelmann turned one hundred in 1999 she offered this lesson about life: "Why sit down and moan about your aches and pains? Even though my time is short, it doesn't bother me. I don't have it on my mind all the time."

This longtime Savannahian is as sharp as a tack and remembers the tiniest details of a remarkable life. "In 1910, my mother took me to the window to see Halley's comet," said Mildred, who also watched the Great Savannah Races. But perhaps her earliest recollection is watching horse-drawn funeral processions on Anderson Street heading for Laurel Grove Cemetery. She has a "vivid memory" of a white horse in the procession being spooked and rearing back on its hind legs.

Mildred's father operated a grocery store at the corner of 32nd and what was then West Broad Street and the family lived upstairs. She can still recite a childhood rhyme: "From East Broad to West Broad, from Anderson to Bay, if you don't like our limits, you need not play."

She has never been on an airplane (she prefers to remain on "terra firma") but has enjoyed many trips by boat and rail. "You see so much more on a train," she said. Some of those journeys were on the Tybee train for Sunday school picnics at the beach.

Mildred was baptized September 10, 1899, at the Lutheran Church of the Ascension. She was parish secretary for more than seventeen years and for decades was active with the young people's Luther League.

In 1909, Mildred's father closed the grocery store and the family boarded an ocean liner bound for Germany, a voyage that took two weeks. "The man who owned the building [where the grocery store was] wanted it back," she explained. "That's when Papa decided to go back to Germany." At that time the family included Mildred and her sister, Adelina. Their brother, William, was born later. "We left in April and came back to Savannah at the end of September," she said. While in Germany, Mildred "rode bicycles all around the countryside" with her cousins.

Years ago Elise Furse posed on a stuffed dog at Tybee. *Courtesy of Elise Furse.*

When the Gartelmanns returned to Savannah, her father opened another grocery store near 33rd and East Broad Streets. Again, as was customary in those days, the family lived upstairs. It was from the second-story porch that Mildred and other family members looked south and saw the racecars zoom along Victory Drive. She also has fond memories of playing in a dry ditch that ran along 37th Street where, in the spring, wild violets bloomed.

When the Titanic went down in 1912, Mildred was in bed for twenty-one days with typhoid fever. "Papa brought me the newspapers and I read all about it," she said. That also was the year her father purchased a summer home at Vernonburg. At first, the family didn't own a car and took a circuitous route to Vernonburg, riding the streetcar to Sandfly and renting a boat for the remainder of the trip.

Later, Mildred's father bought a car so the family could drive to Vernonburg. At least once, Mildred and several others, including W.B. Spann Sr.—who was in his seventies—walked from 32nd and East Broad to Dancy Avenue. She even has photographs of the memorable trip.

After graduating from Savannah High School, Mildred began work as a stenographer and bookkeeper for Cecil Cheves's insurance business on the tenth floor of the Savannah Bank & Trust Co. building. "I started at ten dollars a week and gave my mother five dollars a week for board," she said.

First published in 1999 in the Morning News.

Irish Nun Recalls Arrival
in Savannah

For Sister Amabilis Nelligan and a handful of other Irish Sisters of Mercy, St. Patrick's Day means attending Mass at the Mercy Convent, watching the parade on television, eating a special dinner at midday and receiving "company" later in the day.

Years ago, when Sister Amabilis was teaching math and science at St. Vincent's Academy, she would attend Mass at St. Patrick's Catholic Church on West Broad Street and watch the parade from a platform on the Bull Street side of the Knights of Columbus hall.

In those days, city and county officials who weren't riding in the parade watched the proceedings from the veranda of the old DeSoto Hotel.

"St. Patrick's Day started out very nice in Savannah," Sister Amabilis said. "We had none of this nonsense that goes on today."

Somehow or another "paper cups began to appear" and the celebration has gone downhill ever since, she said. "But the parade committee is trying to do something about that and I commend them for that."

Sister Amabilis came to this country from County Kerry, Ireland, in 1924 when she was seventeen. "I was one in a large group of Irish girls who came to do missionary work," she explained.

The Irish nuns streamed into the Savannah area between 1922 and 1929 and went on to teach in Georgia, Alabama, Maryland and other states.

Times have changed since Sister Amabilis was a young girl in Ireland observing St. Patrick's Day by attending Mass. "It's a very religious holiday in Ireland," she said. "There's none of the carousing that goes on here."

Sister Amabilis (her name means amiable in Latin) earned her degree at Catholic University in Washington, D.C., and taught in Savannah at St. Vincent's from 1934 to 1944, from 1951 to 1958 and from 1966 to 1972.

"I never taught any boys in Savannah," she said. "The only men I know are the ones whose wives went to St. Vincent's."

In between the years she taught at St. Vincent's, Sister Amabilis taught at St. Pius X in Atlanta and was "in charge" for a few years at St. Mary's

Home for Children. She also taught at Catholic schools in Alabama, Maryland and Pennsylvania.

"We kept the Catholic faith alive in this neck of the woods," she said.

When Sister Amabilis retired from teaching in 1972 she worked at the Rose of Sharon Apartments, where she watched the St. Patrick's Day festivities from the higher floors of the building.

In the evening, young men on their way to the Hibernian Society banquet would drop by the apartments to show their grandmothers how handsome they looked in their tuxedoes, she said.

This St. Patrick's Day she'll be content watching the festivities from afar.

First published in 1990 in the Evening Press.

Friends Bid Arthur
Brannen Farewell

Whether he was clowning around in Johnson Square or knitting a cast net on the side of the LaRoche Avenue causeway to Isle of Hope, the late Arthur Brannen loved to entertain and liked to sketch. When he selected a subject to draw, Arthur would carefully examine it from various angles and, like a golfer lining up a putt, he would stick his arm straight out, squint one eye and give a thumbs up to achieve the proper perspective. Once he showed a buddy a finished drawing and a thumb was smack dab in the middle. Another time he sketched a building at Bethesda Home for Boys and put two big feet in the center.

"That was Arthur," said Albert Hucks, who first knew Arthur as a "Bethesda boy" in the 1930s. "You took him for what he was or you didn't take him at all."

Albert and others gathered last week at Bethesda's Whitefield Chapel to remember the man they described as "reflective," "thoughtful," "intelligent" and a "very, very special man." The tales of Arthur brought laughter and a few tears to the one hundred or so mourners who paid their respects to their "one of a kind" friend.

Arthur—the bearded gentleman often seen around town riding a bicycle while wearing a jumpsuit and white rubber boots—actually died of natural causes more than a year ago in Jacksonville, Florida, according to his death certificate. He would have been eighty-three last July 27.

Arthur had plenty of guardian angels, including Betty Richards, who had known him all her life. Betty's husband, Glaen, like Arthur, grew up at Bethesda. Betty feared the worst when Arthur didn't show up for the 2004 St. Patrick's Day Parade or Bethesda's alumni celebration the following month. She started asking around and heard all kinds of stories.

Eventually she discovered he had died April 22, 2004, at Shands Hospital in Jacksonville. She received a copy of his death certificate,

Arthur Brannen was one of the city's most colorful characters. *Courtesy of the* Savannah Morning News.

which included bits of information that authorities may have found on one of Arthur's homemade business cards. A Jacksonville mortician told her that Arthur was cremated and, when no one claimed the ashes, the police disposed of them.

Childhood friend Fred O'Berry loved Arthur like a brother. "We had a lot of good times together…I miss ole Arthur," who simply liked to entertain people, Fred said, choked with emotion. "He liked to see them laugh."

I interviewed Arthur in 1989 in Johnson Square, where he told me a little bit about his life. He was nine when he went to Bethesda, after having spent most of his early years at the King's Daughters Day Nursery. His mother died when he was two and he didn't see his father until the day his father was buried.

Arthur was a teenager at Bethesda when someone came in and said, "Get your clothes on. You're going to your daddy's funeral," Arthur recalled.

A few years later, Arthur joined the Marines and was mentioned in a narrative called *Brothers in Battle*. "By this time, one tank had run through the Second Platoon position, running over Private First Class Brannen and straddling him and his flamethrower. However, he rose up behind it and was mainly responsible for its destruction."

Arthur fell in love with an Australian nurse; something happened and life never was the same for Arthur after that. That day in the square

Arthur told me he wore white boots so the tops of his feet wouldn't get sunburned. Among the items in his ubiquitous buckets were spare batteries, an extra toothbrush and a Bible with his name imprinted in gold on the cover.

At the memorial service, Bethesda Executive Director David Tribble recalled how several years ago Arthur hit a line drive during a Bethesda alumni softball game. Arthur took off for first base and kept on going down the right field line and into the woods.

Harold Branam told how he would often bump into Arthur in Thunderbolt and environs, where he spent most of his last years. Harold would be hurrying to work and Arthur wanted to take the time to chat. Looking back, he said, Arthur was "showing us how to live."

"He was a nonconformist who lived his life the way he wanted to," Harold said, comparing Arthur to Henry David Thoreau. "I'll miss having Arthur around to tell us the meaning of life."

Several folks who told stories about Arthur insisted that he was not a panhandler or moocher. Vincent Russo described him as a "big-hearted" character who was always trying to teach, whether it was how to tie knots in a cast net or how to take the time to relax. Vincent said he regretted not taking a picture of Arthur the last time he saw him. He was giving Arthur a ride in his boat and Arthur was in his element, sitting there with the wind in his hair and a flag in the background.

Lyndy Brannen, who was Arthur's second cousin, believes that Arthur taught others to accept people who "don't fit into the mold."

Toward the end of the service Betty turned on a taped "interview" with Arthur that was conducted several years ago by Jack Diamond. Arthur played a couple of tunes on his harmonica and added his own ending when Jack asked him to say something. Arthur, in turn, sang his response, belting out the first few words of "Let Me Call You Sweetheart."

Later the Bethesda Alumni Society received a copy of a more detailed coroner's report that said Arthur went to the emergency room at Shands Hospital on April 11, 2004, complaining of chest pains. Four days later he underwent angioplasty. Apparently complications occurred and another heart procedure was planned, but delayed because of his condition. While recuperating he evidently told healthcare providers that he planned to continue rowing his boat to Key West.

Sadly, Arthur never made it; death came a few days later. But as one friend said, he died doing exactly what he wanted to do. Plus, he was in the hospital being taken care of and didn't die on the street.

A few months ago, after word of his death circulated locally, a few of Arthur's friends from Colonel's Island e-mailed me with questions. One said she deeply regretted his passing. "I've had the pleasure of talking to Arthur through the years at Yellow Bluff Fishing Camp. He would stay [down here] for three to four weeks. Usually he could be making a cast net for somebody."

While in the Midway area, Arthur would often attend Midway United Methodist Church, where he would sit in the front row and sing loudly (albeit a little off key).

First published in 2005 in the Morning News.

Love of Dance Has Spawned a Lifetime of Friends, Memories

Madeleine Walker has two children of her own and hundreds of others who are like her own: youngsters who, years ago, attended her Little Folks School and current and former students who danced at her ballet school.

"I love it or I wouldn't be here," she said one recent busy afternoon while sitting behind the desk at her bustling ballet studio. "I feel like everyone in this studio is like family."

While we chatted, parents streamed in to purchase recital tickets and little girls in black leotards and pink tights hurried in to classes taught by Madeleine's daughter, Natalie Deriso, and Gaye Baxley Hadaway. Night classes are handled by Ann Inglis.

A few weeks ago, the former Jennifer Grissette (who left Madeleine and Savannah to dance professionally) was home from Germany for a visit. One of Jennifer's first stops—with her five-month-old twin girls in tow—was Madeleine's studio, where the walls are filled with countless photos of former students like Jennifer. Also on the wall is an endearing poem entitled "The Ballet Mistress," which was penned by former student Melissa Sydeman who, in part, described Madeleine this way:

> Her hoarse voice rasped out words we danced but could not read; twelve girls whose toes turned out each time she said, "plies"…Madeleine at 60. Still her ageless, olive skin stretched smooth. Stately still, her toe shoes echoed past the arabesques.

Like any proud mother, Madeleine is delighted with her students' accomplishments and the generations of Savannahians she has taught. "I guess the most satisfaction comes when students come back with their children," she explained.

And there are plenty, beginning with both boys and girls who, in the early 1940s, came to Madeleine's kindergarten at the corner of Victory Drive and Skidaway Road.

The Little Folks School, as it was called, was a Hansel-and-Gretel-like cottage where Madeleine was "Miss Madeleine." She picked up the children in a station wagon that had a horn that played "Rock a Bye Baby."

By then, Madeleine also was teaching ballet in the afternoon. She started taking lessons when she was seven and was fortunate to study in New York.

"Mother [Marguerite "Mimi" Thompson] was always into voice," she recalled. "She sang in every church choir in Savannah. She'd go to Mass and then go on to other churches. She even sang at the synagogue."

In the summer Madeleine's mother would travel to New York with Madeleine by her side. While her mother studied voice, Madeleine took ballet. (In later years Mimi, who died when she was ninety-six, often answered the phone at the studio and sewed ribbons on hundreds of toe shoes.)

At home, Madeleine continued her ballet under the direction of women like Dorothy Bacon, one of her favorites.

After finishing St. Vincent's Academy, Madeleine returned to New York to study ballet. Ironically, that's how she became interested in kindergarten work. Madeleine's practical father supported her efforts but didn't believe she could make a living as a professional dancer. Like many parents of that era, Mr. Thompson encouraged Madeleine to become a schoolteacher. (Her brother Jack Thompson was a football coach at Benedictine.)

Madeleine bowed to her father's advice and, in 1940, opened the Little Folks School. But she also taught ballet in the afternoons at her studio in the Savannah Hotel. She continued for a few years until she was married and briefly moved away. (The quaint little kindergarten later became the popular Our House Restaurant.)

Madeleine returned to Savannah when her husband, John, was overseas. She helped teach ballet at a local studio and took a respite for a few years with her two daughters, Madeleine Walker Perry and Natalie.

Madeleine operated a studio at the old Jefferson Athletic Club at Lincoln and 35th Streets before the early 1950s, when she moved to her present location at Waters Avenue and 50th Street.

Baby boomers may remember when Madeleine offered ballroom dancing as well as ballet. She was prompted by parents who were anxious for their pre-adolescents and teenagers to learn the rumba or the foxtrot.

"Right now those men can really dance," she said.

Through the years, Madeleine became friends with various other local teachers and established the Savannah Ballet Guild with Rosalie Cotler and Doris Martin.

First published in 1999 in the Morning News.

Author Fascinated by
Story of Black Nun

A few years ago author Gail Karwoski stumbled across the story of the late Matilda Beasley of Savannah and just couldn't let go.

She ended up nominating Beasley to Georgia Women of Achievement, a nonprofit organization that honors women who made extraordinary contributions to society. Beasley joined forty-one other women with Savannah connections, including Flannery O'Connor, Juliette Gordon Low, Lucy Barrow McIntire, Mary Musgrove Bosomworth, Anna Colquitt Hunter and Ellen Louise Axson Wilson, who married Woodrow Wilson in June 1885 at Independent Presbyterian Church.

"[Matilda Beasley] was such an amazing character," Gail said.

Gail lives near Athens and writes historical fiction books for children. Her most recent effort by Peachtree Publishers is *Seamen: The Dog Who Explored the West With Lewis and Clark*. She is the coauthor of *The Tree That Owns Itself and Other Adventure Tales From Out of the Past*.

While doing research several years ago Gail read about Beasley, who became the first black nun in Georgia. In 1889 she founded the first black community of Religious Sisters in Georgia: the Sisters of the Third Order of St. Francis.

Two years earlier Beasley had established the St. Francis Home for Colored Orphans in Savannah, near Sacred Heart Catholic Church. Around the turn of the last century the home was moved to East Broad and Gaston Streets. A park on the site is named in her honor.

I wrote a story about Mother Beasley, as she was called, in 1992 when Savannah City Council voted to name the park in the nun's honor. Beasley's story already had caught the attention of Sister Charlene Walsh when she was planning a Georgia Day program at St. Benedict's Catholic Church. She collected a thick folder of materials on the nun's life and her contributions to the Church and Savannah's black community.

During the 1850s and 1860s Mother Beasley taught black children in her home when it was illegal to do so. Her husband died in 1878, leaving her his property and belongings. She in turn gave the property to the Catholic Church to be used for the poor.

When Mother Beasley died in 1903 her funeral Mass was held at Sacred Heart and was crowded with Protestants and Catholics and both black and white mourners.

First published in 2002 in the Morning News.

Myrtice Price Was
Caring Gould Cottage Director

Myrtice Price figures a book called *Daddy Long Legs* made her fall in love with the idea of working with children. The novel tells the story of an orphan girl who lived a charmed life thanks to an anonymous benefactor.

Myrtice, ninety-two, wasn't an orphan, but simply liked that heartwarming tale of long ago. In 1933 she began teaching kindergarten at the Gould Cottage on East 54th Street. The cottage was a children's home established by Edwin Gould, a wealthy, kind-hearted New Yorker who had a lavish home on nearby Jekyll Island and a deep affection for Savannah and children.

From 1940 to 1958 Myrtice was director of the children's home. The Gould Cottage came into existence shortly after Edwin Gould visited the Savannah Female Orphan Asylum on West Broad Street. (The orphan asylum later was known as the Savannah Home for Girls and was relocated to 54th Street, where both it and the Gould Cottage were havens for children from troubled or broken homes.)

Gould "saw the need for a place for small children and, out of the goodness of his heart, bought part of the old polo field [on 54th]," she explained.

The Gould Cottage opened in 1933 for forty children from about age five to ten. "The King's Daughters were operating a nursery on Montgomery Street and there was the Savannah Home and Bethesda for older children but nothing in between," Myrtice said.

Myrtice served as director of the home from 1940 to 1958. She has many fond memories of the Gould Cottage, including her wedding there in 1949.

Some cases, she admitted, were sad, because "no matter what, [children] clung to their homes." But, she added, "it was rewarding for us to know we were taking care of the children no matter how short-term the stay might be."

If Myrtice has one regret, it's not knowing what happened to all the children who passed through the doors of the Gould Cottage.

"I've always been sorry I didn't keep a personal record of all those children," she said.

The Gould Cottage was a haven for children. *Courtesy of the* Savannah Morning News.

After I profiled Myrtice Price, I received a call from a woman who wanted to track down a woman who took care of her and her sister when they lived at the Gould Cottage. This is her story.

Faye Bragg Holsten is especially grateful this Thanksgiving because she has found an angel of a woman who watched over her when she was a toddler at the Gould Cottage.

"My sister [Martha] and I had always wanted to find [the woman] and thank her for the loving care she gave us," Faye said.

Although she was then just a toddler, Faye recalled a "kind and gentle woman" rocking her at night and tucking her in a small bed beside her own. For breakfast the woman would fix oatmeal sweetened with maple syrup for Faye and Martha, and the other children at the Gould Cottage.

It was 1940 and Faye was one of the first babies placed at the children's home. Faye's parents had divorced and her mother had gained custody of Faye and Martha. After "many hardships" and struggles, their mother placed the little girls in the Gould Cottage.

Faye telephoned to tell me all this after she read a recent column I wrote about Myrtice Price, who was director of the Gould Cottage from 1940–1958. Faye was anxious to get in touch with Mrs. Price because she wanted to know what happened to the kind woman she remembered as Mrs. Heath.

Faye jotted down her thoughts of that moment: "As I read the article, it brought back many memories shared by my sister and me. I phoned Polly to thank her for writing the story, but what I was really interested in was getting Mrs. Price's phone number. When I mentioned that a Mrs. Heath had taken care of us, Polly told me that Mrs. Price was a Heath before she married Mr. Price in 1949.

"My heart began to beat faster as I realized that a lifelong dream was about to take place," Faye said.

Faye and Martha already had found their mother—45 years after she left them at the Gould Cottage. The girls stayed at the home for three years until their father, the late Battey Bragg, got out of the service and remarried. Faye and Martha were devoted to their stepmother, Tita Bragg, but they had questions that only their mother could answer. Faye began searching for her mother when she was in her 40s after giving birth to her last child.

"I thought then, 'How can a mother leave her baby and not wonder?'" she said.

"At first, she didn't want anything to do with us," Faye said. "We sent pictures and wrote letters, and finally after three years my sister and I decided we really needed to go."

Faye remembers arriving at the retirement home and hearing her mother coming down the hall saying to the home's director, "Why did they come? I didn't want them to come."

When their mother saw them, she was polite and gracious, Faye said. "There was no bond, but we were able to fill in the gaps that needed to be filled in. The main thing was that we had questions answered."

Six months later their mother was diagnosed with cancer and died.

Now Faye and Martha have found the angel who watched over them at the Gould Cottage.

Not too long ago, the two women visited and reminisced with Mrs. Price, who said it made her feel good "to think I had a little part in the girls turning out the way they did."

All those years ago Faye remembers "Mrs. Heath" dressing them up in their best clothes on Sunday. "My sister always held my hand because she didn't want us to be separated," Faye said.

"We'd go outside and hang onto the fence to watch familiar faces coming from the streetcar," she said. If relatives couldn't visit, "Mrs. Heath would take us over to a blanket on the ground, give us candy and read stories to us."

The visit with Mrs. Price was priceless, Faye said. "She held us tightly and we all wept together."

First published in 1998 in the Morning News.

A Father's Bitterness Over
War Lives Forever

Inscribed, in part, on the imposing granite marker in the small graveyard near Bloomingdale are angry words: "The incompetent, greedy, confused politicians…were responsible for this boy being murdered."

These words were etched on the marker after Marine PFC James Waring Horning Jr. was killed in action at Yudam-Ni, Chosin Reservoir, Korea. Horning's father, nicknamed "Judge," ordered the huge memorial after he learned of his only son's death. The elder Horning already had lost a wife and a daughter, friends said.

Every war, including the one being fought in Iraq, has its critics, many of whom are much more vocal than others.

For Judge Horning, the anger and bitterness lives forever on the large lump of granite that stands near his son's grave. The younger Horning, who turned nineteen that fall, arrived in Korea on November 11, 1950. In a letter penned to then-Senator Walter F. George of Georgia, Judge Horning pleaded for help to bring his son home. In it he wrote: "My son is very precious to me…the war in Korea was not, I feel, his fight; he should never have been in it and could never benefit by it. I believe the only chance to get him out of Korea is to use the atom bomb…will you help save my boy's life? America needs him and the others who are in Korea."

The *Morning News* received a copy of the letter on December 8, 1950, just two days before a devastated Judge Horning was notified by telegram that his son had been killed in action on December 2.

Betty Eason Vickery, who had known the younger Horning since the fifth grade, remembers Judge Horning being "very bitter" about his son's death. When Chosin Reservoir veteran Jim McAleer wrote a book about Dog Company, Betty shared with him some of the letters that she received from her longtime friend. In one, Horning wrote that he was sitting on a mountaintop looking down on the Chosin Reservoir. He said he would have plenty of stories to tell when he returned.

"We all thought he was coming home," Betty recalled. Sadly, she received news of his death while she was socializing with a group of teenagers at the community center in Bloomingdale.

In *Out of Savannah, Dog Company, USMCR*, McAleer wrote that Horning would never again fish in the Ogeechee River and would be "forever 19."

On August 21, 1950, Dog Company was activated and ordered to Korea. Like many young patriotic-minded men, Horning had joined the Marine Corps Reserve in the late 1940s.

Harrell Roberts was another one of those 182 men who joined Dog Company. "It was right after World War II," he recalled. "Who would've thought that there would be another war?"

The reservists in Dog Company drilled in Forsyth Park and went to summer camp for two weeks. On August 21, 1950, the company was activated and ordered to Korea.

For the big send-off, crowds gathered and the Parris Island Marine Band played as the men marched from the park to the Central of Georgia Railroad depot. From there they boarded a train to Camp Pendleton, California, where they received twenty-four days of training before boarding a ship. They arrived in Korea on November 11, 1950.

Roberts was wounded on December 1, the day before Horning died.

Longtime county residents may remember that the marker ordered by Judge Horning stood for many years in Bloomingdale alongside U.S. 80. When the highway was widened, Roberts said, the marker was moved to the stretch of Bloomingdale Road between Interstate 16 and U.S. 80. Later, the imposing piece of granite was relocated to Gravel Hill Cemetery.

First published in 2004 in the Morning News.

Mitchell Saw and Heard It All
at the Golf Club

Hamilton Mitchell has plenty of memories of the folks who frequented the Savannah Golf Club during the thirty-five years he worked there. The names mentioned by Mitchell, as he prefers to be called, sound like a Who's Who of the city's movers and shakers.

Mitchell began his tour of duty at the Golf Club just after World War II. He was an experienced employee, having worked at the John Wesley Hotel coffee shop and as an elevator operator in the Savannah Bank and Trust Co. building. In the mid-1940s, Mitchell was working at a shipyard when he decided to apply at the Golf Club.

"I was working at Southeastern Shipyard and Mr. Henry Dunn knew it was going to be phased out," Mitchell recalled. "He insisted I go to the Golf Club."

In those days, the grand old Southern-style clubhouse was tucked under a canopy of pines on Gwinnett Street near Wheaton Street. The top floor of the clubhouse was for men only. The second-floor locker room, smoking room and bar "wasn't pretty, but it was like home," Mitchell said.

If a member needed golf shoes cleaned or something else taken care of, they'd turn to Mitchell, who offered services with a smile.

And Mitchell was always around to witness the shenanigans that went on after golf rounds, including the hoots and hollers that began when some of the guys gave hole-by-hole commentaries of their missed putts, chips and drives.

"I'm telling you, there were some characters out there," Mitchell said, rolling his eyes and laughing.

When Mitchell answered the phone, he did it with his unmistakable, staccato greeting, "Golf Club." But sometimes answering the phone put Mitchell on the spot. A member's wife might be on the other end asking for her husband, possibly preparing to chew him out for being late.

Mitchell would look out into the smoke-filled card room, spot the member and ask, "Is so-and-so here?" The member might shake his head and wave his hands as if to say, "Protect me, Mitchell, tell her I'm not here."

And Mitchell always came through for his men.

In 1960 or so, when the new clubhouse was built on President Street, Mitchell and longtime club employee Charlie Marks went along. "We tried real hard to give it our best," Mitchell said. Instead of working in the locker room at the new club, Mitchell was transferred "up front," where he was supervisor of service.

Mitchell decided to retire a few years ago when the "hours were getting too long." Sometimes he'd work from 8:00 a.m. to 3:00 a.m. "My feet were giving out on me," he explained.

Nowadays, Mitchell is a familiar face as a bartender at private parties, where he often runs into folks he knew at the Golf Club.

First published in 1989 in the Evening Press.

Veteran Storyteller
Entertains Us on Vacation

Exactly what was the familial setup of that 1950s television sitcom *The Real McCoys*? There was Grandpappy Amos, of course, and grandson Luke and his wife, Kate. But who were Little Luke and Hassie? They weren't Luke and Kate's children, were they?

And what about the Clampetts of *The Beverly Hillbillies*? What happened to Jed's wife, who was Ellie May's mother? And why did Jethro live with the family?

These are the kinds of thought-provoking questions my sisters and I wrestled with recently during a weeklong vacation.

When we weren't watching sitcoms like *The Real McCoys* or *The Andy Griffith Show*—my eyes actually filled with tears during a Christmas episode—we braved the heat and went swimming or bicycling.

The best part of the vacation, by far, was sitting around the supper table listening to my father, Dr. Leander Powers, talk about what it was like growing up in Guyton, the tiny Effingham County town where he was born.

Years ago, Guyton was considered a resort and, believe it or not, was home to three hotels that were like second homes for many Savannahians. They could catch a train that came through Guyton several times a day. "I never wore a watch because I could tell what time it was by which particular train was going through," Daddy said.

When he was in the seventh grade, Daddy rode the train to Savannah to take saxophone lessons from a man who lived on West 41st Street. "I'd get off at the depot and catch the streetcar," he recalled. This was during Prohibition, but the music teacher managed to have plenty of liquor on hand, which didn't sit too well with my grandmother, who many people knew as Miss Maggie.

"He'd line up his liquor bottles on the mantel," Daddy recalled. "I remember one time Mama asked him why he didn't quit drinking," my father said. "He said he just couldn't and she told him the Lord would help

At one time, streetcars ran along Broughton Street. *Courtesy of the* Savannah Morning News.

him do anything." The music teacher looked at my grandmother and asked point blank, "'Mrs. Powers? Can the Lord hold twelve eels in his hand?'"

My grandmother, who never was at a loss for words, had no reply.

Later, when my father graduated from high school, he and his father, brother and other family members drove to Chicago in a 1934 Ford. Along for the ride was Daddy's good buddy Carl Hodges, who was the only other boy in his class all through school in Guyton. (There were seven people in the class.)

Once they arrived on the outskirts of Chicago, Daddy and Carl decided to go to town to see a burlesque show. "We went in around 4:30 and I believe we watched it twice," Daddy recalled.

"When we came out it was dark and we had no idea where we were. We were walking down the street and I was thinking about [John] Dillinger getting shot when all the sudden a man tapped me on the shoulder and asked for a cigarette. I gave him the whole pack and we hopped on the streetcar. We didn't know where it was going but we wanted out of there."

That wasn't all the excitement the Guyton group experienced on the Chicago trip. On the way home they were involved in a head-on collision near Morristown, Tennessee.

"My head was cut so we had to go into town to get stitches," Daddy said. "We also hired a lawyer and when we got back to the car some crooked mountaineer had pushed it across the county line into a town called McBean. The lawyer said the best thing for us to do was to see if [they] would give us a tire. We got the car fixed and got out of town as fast as we could."

Sounds like Daddy's stories would rival those on *The Real McCoys* or *The Andy Griffith Show*.

First published in 1999 in the Morning News.

Aunts Like Lillian "Cookie" Nussbaum Were Special

For many fortunate folks, an aunt is the next best thing to a grandmother or mother. In my case, I had ten aunts, including two who had no children and loved nothing better than to dote on their nieces and nephews. These two aunts, the late Lillie May Perkins and Frances "Auntie" Cooke, were schoolteachers who for years taught many a child in various schools around town.

To me they were sweet ladies who always offered a kiss, a tight hug and a treat when I visited.

I've often wondered why the greeting card companies haven't come up with "Aunt's Day," since there's a designated day for most everybody else. Since the card folks haven't done it, I hereby designate February 27 as "Aunt's Day" for all the adored aunts who have made our lives better.

Another of those special women was Lillian Nussbaum, aunt to Walt Nussbaum and great-aunt to Kemp Nussbaum and Jane Nussbaum Stanley.

Walt Nussbaum's Aunt Lil was a former teacher and principal, "a wonderful person who touched many lives through her love of family and her love of education."

Kemp said he is asked "all the time" if he is related to the Miss Nussbaum who taught school. "Interestingly enough, they would always tell me how strict she was and how she demanded respect. Yet this is the same lady who spoiled me rotten."

For Kemp and Jane, their Aunt Lil never missed a birthday or significant milestone in their lives. "In fact she would always take us anywhere we wanted to eat for our birthdays," he recalled. "What I remember most about those dinners is her playing 'I Spy' and the hot fudge sundaes at Shoney's. She was always there and, in her mind, we were individually the most perfect people on earth."

For as long as Kemp and Jane remember, Lil lived in Fort Wayne Apartments in Trustees Gardens. She grew roses and kept a crystal candy jar on the table next to her chair. In later years she had a live-in sitter.

Everyday she and the sitter would pull up to Kemp's house and "Lil would send the sitter in to ask what she could buy us for dinner."

She would always bring cookies for the neighborhood children, who referred to her as "Cookie." "She would just smile and hand the bag of cookies out the window to all the kids," Kemp said. "She would sit and watch them play until they would have to go inside. Come to think of it, she was the last kid to go home many nights."

When Lil was in her late eighties, Jane opened a retail shop in Trustees Gardens, around the corner from her great-aunt's apartment. After she picked up her daughter Kara from preschool, Kara would go over to Lil's and have an ice cream float and watch *Sesame Street* with her.

"Lil's biggest fear was being alone when she died," Jane said. "One morning I got a call from her sitter. Lil was not doing well and she had called an ambulance. I locked up and ran around the corner to her apartment. She was in her favorite chair (with the candy jar full on the table) and struggling with her breath. I threw my arms around her and told her I was there and she wasn't alone. She took one more breath and passed on."

Several days after Lil's funeral, Jane's daughters asked to go to Bonaventure Cemetery. "The whole time we were there a butterfly fluttered around us," Jane said. "It gave me a beautiful example of death for the girls. I thought to myself, 'Lil is still keeping an eye on her family.'"

First published in 2005 in the Morning News.

Fans Remember
"Daddy-O of the Radio"

Growing up with older sisters who are nine and eleven years my senior meant that I was introduced to various rites of passage for teenagers who grew up in Savannah in the late 1950s and early '60s.

One of those experiences as a tagalong was bouncing along Victory Drive in the backseat of a ghostly gray 1949 Dodge and listening to a now-defunct AM radio station called WBYG.

When I read Mel Mixon's name in the newspaper's obituary column I momentarily reached back to those childhood days.

The newspaper appears on my front lawn every morning but I generally check out the online version of the *Morning News*, which is at www.savannahnow.com. I found Mixon's obit and clicked onto the guestbook, which is similar to the book friends sign at the funeral home, church or synagogue. This computer version, however, is all done in cyberspace so folks from all over the United States and world can e-mail their condolences to bereaved families.

One of those who sent a message to Mel Mixon's family was Charles Varner of Hilton Head Island, South Carolina, who described Mel as a "remarkable entertainment figure" for the youth of Savannah.

When I asked Charles to elaborate he told me he worked part time at the Lucas Theatre from June 1960 to June 1962.

"Because Mel's station, WSGA, did advertising for the Lucas, we sent the station plenty of free passes each month," Charles recalled. "Our friend, Mel, visited often…He was not only a highly talented radio personality, possessing the golden voice as well as excellent technical expertise, but was also one of the mature deejays who didn't take himself too seriously."

Longtime Savannah radio personality Danny Kramer of Salt Lake City offered this message: "When I was a young pup and just beginning my career, I almost literally sat at Mel's knee and even tried to emulate his delivery [but] never did it half as good.

"I'm truly sorry to see that Mel isn't here now, but no doubt he is entertaining the young angels in heaven."

Jan New-Wrightson of Lancaster, New Hampshire, said she "spent many a night listening to Mel's melodious voice on WSGA and at the Our House [restaurant] parking lot."

Larry Usry Sr. of Metter remembers "waiting each night with my transistor radio for the theme tune, 'Movin,' and the entertainment provided by the Daddy-O of the Radio."

James Bigbie of Savannah believes "God is surely putting together a great radio station. Mel will be missed on Earth, but his golden voice will not be forgotten. Mel has joined the likes of [DJ] Bruce Lapp and many other greats."

Jackie Ray of Midway said, "watching and listening to [Mel] at Our House seems like yesterday."

Dean Evans of Springfield worked at WSGA with Mixon and Kramer in 1964, "cueing up the old Shoney's commercials and other things around the station. Mel, Danny, Dot and I, and two or three others all made up the 'Serendipity Singers.' (Remember, 'Ah hah, oh no don't let the rain come down?')"

He added this message for the unforgettable DJ: "Mel, I will always remember you sitting in the glassed-in [DJ] booth, above the restaurant on Bay Street spinnin' the discs. You will always be the 'the Daddy-O of the Radio.'"

First published in 2003 in the Evening Press.

In Search of the
Real Clarence Thomas

One day last week a reporter from a national magazine was camped out on the front porch of Leola Williams's East 32nd Street home, patiently waiting for the mother of Supreme Court nominee Clarence Thomas. Meanwhile, at Candler Hospital, where Leola has worked for fourteen years, the telephone in the community relations office was ringing off the hook.

"Everybody was looking for Leola," said Midge Schildkraut, manager of public relations at Candler.

Reporters from national magazines, newspapers and television programs were swarming around Leola, interviewing her about her son's life in Savannah and poring over childhood snapshots of the man who may become the nation's next Supreme Court Justice.

The list of media people who talked with Leola read like the newspaper rack in the library: *Time*, *People*, *USA Today*, the *Washington Post*, the *Chicago Tribune*, the *Baltimore Sun* and more.

As one reporter was overheard saying, a la Andy Warhol, "She's having her fifteen minutes of fame."

The reporters were looking for Leola and any smidgeon of background information they could dig up on her son. They wanted to find the Pinpoint community where Thomas was born. They wanted to delve into Thomas's past at the Catholic schools he attended and see the church where he was an altar boy.

Most days at Candler, Midge handles three or four calls from the local media. "We usually have a few calls, but nothing like this," she said. "It was a deluge." Thomas's sister, Emma Mae Martin, also works at Candler, a fact that did not escape reporters wanting interviews.

And everybody wanted directions to Pinpoint so they could bounce along the dusty roads and talk to people like Helen Johnson, who has lived in the tiny community for seventy-five years.

"Is that called a savanna?" one reporter asked, pointing to the marsh at

Supreme Court Justice Clarence Thomas greets his good friend Betty Purdy. *Courtesy of the* Savannah Morning News.

Pinpoint. "Is this a grove of oaks?" Sometimes it takes patience in dealing with the out-of-towners.

Just ask Leola.

"Leola needed her own secretary," a nurse said. "Every time the phone rang it was for Leola."

At the Catholic Pastoral Center on Liberty Street, Father William Simmons also was fielding calls from the national media. He dug up a couple of Thomas's yearbooks from the chancery and marked the pages on which pictures of Thomas appear.

We'll probably see those pictures and articles over and over again in the next few months. Some will make us cringe and others will make us laugh, but we know the untold story of how proud we are that Judge Clarence Thomas calls Savannah home.

First published in 1991 in the Evening Press.

Medicine:
The Way It Used To Be

Those who can remember the old DeSoto Hotel are sure to recall the rocking chair fleet, the corner beauty parlor and Dr. William V. Long's office on the Liberty Street side.

Dr. Long was hotel doctor for thirty-eight years. He also treated guests at the General Oglethorpe Hotel on Wilmington Island and at the DeSoto Beach Motel. On top of all that, he saw private patients as well.

Being a hotel doctor back then was interesting but tiring because, basically, Dr. Long was on call all the time. "One thing I didn't like was the late afternoon and evening work and being on duty twenty-four hours a day," Dr. Long said.

Dr. Long, who practiced in Savannah from the early 1920s until 1975, accepted the assignment at the DeSoto in 1927, when the hotel doctor accidentally splashed acid in his eyes and lost his sight.

The vice-president and general manager of the DeSoto knew Dr. Long and asked him to take over the job. Dr. Long treated guests for just about everything, including drunkenness.

He recalls sobering up a North Carolina man and sending him on his way to the railroad station, where the man cashed in his train ticket and "bought more liquor and landed back in the hotel."

He even treated celebrities like Andy Griffith, who had the flu while visiting Savannah.

Dr. Long wasn't the only physician in his family. He is a descendant of Dr. Crawford W. Long, who first used ether as an anesthetic. A native of Comer, Dr. Long grew up in Danielsville, where his father was probate judge. He graduated from the University of Georgia and Emory Medical School, where he met Dr. John Elliott, another Savannah physician.

Dr. Long said Dr. Elliott was known as a "walking library" because he always carried books. They roomed together during training at Grady Hospital in Atlanta and are still friends. From Grady, Dr. Long went to Savannah's old St. Joseph's Hospital, where he was an intern.

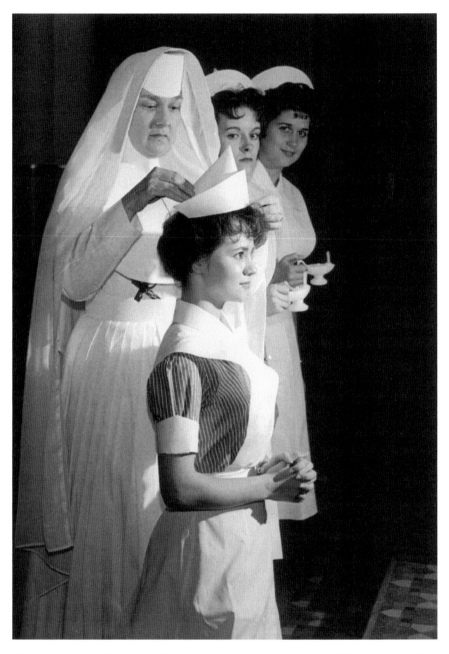

Graduates of the old St. Joseph's Hospital School of Nursing were "capped" by instructors who were members of the Religious Sisters of Mercy. *Courtesy of the* Savannah Morning News.

In those days, hospitals were only 40 percent full because people couldn't afford to be sick, even though rooms were about five dollars a day. If you were admitted as a patient, hospital personnel would "meet you at the door, shake your hand and thank you for coming," Dr. Long said.

Surgery was particularly difficult because there was no air conditioning and fans were prohibited because they stirred up dust. A doctor wearing a cloth gown, mask and cap sweated profusely in the operating room.

"I had a nurse on either side of me wiping the perspiration from my brow," Dr. Long said.

Dr. Long made house calls for two to three dollars and delivered babies for fifty dollars. His practice kept him busy, but he found time to be a city alderman and president of the local chapter of the Georgia Medical Society.

Before his sight began to fail, he enjoyed hunting. In his wallet, he carries a picture of a boat laden with deer that he and his friends shot on Ossabaw Island.

First published in 1989 in the Evening Press.

Part II

Landmarks and Neighborhoods

Simple Pleasures Conjure Up
Precious Memories

The arrival of fall brings magnolias to mind for me, because to this one-time little girl and her pals, those stately beauties were the best climbing trees in the whole world. And back then the crisp days of autumn meant it was time to see who could gather a record number of magnolia seeds.

It was a simple pleasure—one that conjures up precious memories of neighborhood friends like Mary Frances, Mary Lynn, Laura and Linda. When we were growing up in the early 1960s on the fringes of Savannah's Ardsley Park there was no such thing as a video game. Sure, we had televisions with channels 3 and 11, but the outside world was much more inviting.

We delighted in letting our imaginations soar. Most every afternoon when school let out, we'd hop on our bicycles and take off on an adventure through the neighborhood. Our territory offered a little bit of everything: tree-shaded streets to race down, bushes to take shelter in for hide and go seek and magnificent magnolias to climb.

The best climbing trees for us were the ones in the circle park at East 50th and Harmon streets. We were positive the park had an official name but we all knew it as the circle park.

Today the layout of the park remains the same: one magnolia stands in the center, with four others dotted along the outer limits of that wonderful play area. In our heyday, we'd park our bikes in the great expanse of shade underneath the trees and hoist ourselves into our afternoon hideaways.

The best climbing tree, by far, was the one in the center of the park. We staked out certain spots way in the top. From those seats offered by Mother Nature, we would see what we could see.

Climbing so high as to spy the top of nearby Savannah High School was always a challenge. When we got situated, we'd munch on snacks bought at the Parkside Superette where Charlie always said, "Thank you, ma'am," to each giggling little girl.

For a Coca-Cola, we'd pedal to the soda shop and dig out a smattering of change for a drink in a paper cup with ice. Vending machines were nowhere to be seen.

Afterward we would pack up our goodies, usually in the wire basket that hung on my handlebars, and head back to the park. Managing to carry a package of crackers and a drink to the top of a magnolia tree was a challenge, let me tell you, but we always met our goal.

Those who love magnolias look forward to late spring or early summer when the huge white, sweet-smelling blossoms appear against the large, dark green leaves.

Fall was our time, though, when we'd empty our Coke cups and start collecting shiny, red magnolia seeds. A couple of us would claim one side of a tree and the rest would scour the other.

We'd spend hours in those trees, painstakingly gathering seeds. Then, worn out from work, we'd climb down, count our bounty and scatter the seeds throughout the park. The squirrels and birds were guaranteed a feast.

Perhaps those children who spend hours in front of their computers will turn out to be smarter than we are. But I'll wager one hundred red magnolia seeds they aren't having as much fun as we did.

First published in 1994 in the Evening Press.

Contractor Helping Restore
Ailing Ardsley Park Pillars

As a child, Joan Graham Hester Byrd didn't live in Ardsley Park. But she has vivid memories of strolling through the nearby neighborhood with her sister, Betty Graham Hunter, and their aunt, Rubye Graham, who taught for years at Charles Ellis School.

"We thought Ardsley Park was special," Joan recalled.

The Graham girls also had the opportunity to gaze at scores of beautiful Ardsley Park homes when they accompanied their father, Anson Graham, on his regular route for Free Bros. Laundry.

The girls took note of the Belgian block pillars with the terra cotta roofs that defined the Ardsley Park neighborhood. Today some of the remaining pillars, or gates, can still be seen along Bull Street between Victory Drive and East 54th Street. Two are situated on the corner of Washington and Waters Avenues and another is on Victory Drive between Abercorn and Habersham streets.

The majestic-looking gates stand out in Joan's memory.

"We were so aware of their beauty," she recalled. "I remember my aunt pointing them out to us when she took us on walks through there. We thought they were awfully pretty."

Sadly, some of the pillars are gone and only a couple of them still have their orange roofs.

But all that will change, thanks to the efforts of a local builder who plans to restore the pillars.

Omar El-Khalidi, who owns Sterling Builders Inc., decided to take on the project one pillar at a time. He'll start with the one on Victory Drive between Abercorn and Habersham.

"I noticed that one falling into disrepair," he explained. "It kills me to see pieces of tile falling off and stuff [timbers under the roofs] rotting away. I live in Ardsley Park and one day I said to myself, 'Omar, you need to do something.' At some point in our lives we need to chip in and do something for the community."

Omar plans to cast the terra cotta tiles and donate his time and materials. His project has the enthusiastic support of both the Ardsley Park Garden Club and the Ardsley Park Neighborhood Association.

"We think it's wonderful that he is taking the initiative and is willing to share his talents and time," said Kim Ergul of the Ardsley Park Garden Club. "We will do whatever we can to offer our assistance."

Sterling Builders specializes in historic restoration. Omar's projects have included work at the Juliette Gordon Low National Center, Wormsloe Historic Site, the Cathedral of St. John the Baptist and Mercer House, among others.

Joan Byrd was pleased when she heard about Omar's plans to restore the pillars. She had noticed the deterioration and was hoping some individual or organization would pitch in to help.

"Through the years the pillars had gone away, so to speak," she said. "I'm just delighted that someone is finally going to restore them."

After I wrote this column for the Morning News *in 2001, I received a clipping from a helpful reference librarian at the public library. The clipping was from a 1942 edition of the* Savannah Morning News *that said that the "48 iron gates at the entrances to Ardsley Park" would be given as scrap metal to the war cause. "They will be cut up for the use of industries making planes, ships and munitions."*

Tybee Strikes Nostalgic Chord

Spending a bit of time at Tybee always brings back memories of childhood days enjoying the sun and sand with my Atlanta cousins. It was the early 1960s when we would stay at the family-owned Powers Apartments on 17th Street.

I know what I remember about those glory days, but I decided to consult the cousins, whom I haven't seen in thirty years, to find out what they remember about terrific times at Tybee.

I e-mailed Stellise Logan Kirk in Atlanta and her sister, Mae Logan Kelly in Clyde, North Carolina, whose grandmother, the late Louise Powers Robey, was my aunt. Here are snippets of what they sent. I'll use initials (SLK for Stellise; MLK for Mae; and PPS for me):

"The two-story house had no air conditioning and only one black-and-white television in the tiny office in the front where room keys hung from nails on the wall (in between penciled telephone numbers). We didn't watch much TV, though. There were too many other fun things to do." (PPS)

"Coloring in coloring books on the second-floor porch with the beach in view beyond the Cobb's Apartments sign." (SLK)

"Ants in the sugar...roaches scurrying about when we turned on the light in a dark room...the rustle of palmetto branches against the house." (MLK)

"Walking to Strickland's Market on Butler Avenue to pick up the mail." (PPS)

"Sidestepping stickers that grew through the cracks in the asphalt sidewalk and skipping to the beach where we'd pile our towels on the jetties while we went swimming." (PPS)

"Swinging on the boardwalk rails. Polly could go completely around and I was envious that I couldn't." (SLK)

"Chu's Department Store (need I say more?)" (SLK)

"I remember that creepy fortuneteller machine at Chu's similar to the one in the movie *Big* with Tom Hanks." (MLK)

Construction began in 1934 on the Powers House at Tybee. *Courtesy of Dr. L.K. Powers.*

"Granddad [Curry Robey] took us to the 'rides' most every night." (MLK)

"I remember riding the Ferris wheel. We hoped to be lucky enough to be at the very top when the ride stopped to board new riders below. There we were—facing the ocean from atop a Ferris wheel at night with the summer breeze cooling our sunburned faces. Oh! And more than once our flip flops slipped off and sailed away to the crowd below." (SLK)

"I still don't like heights." (PPS)

"At the pavilion stand we'd buy lemon custard ice cream and snow cones so full of syrup that the paper cones would get soggy and drip onto our hands long before we finished." (SLK)

"Mama Lou [my cousins' name for their grandmother] would go beachcombing and bring home towels, Army blankets and other stuff that people left behind." (MLK)

"It was definitely a different time." (PPS)

[Noni Dasher was a frequent guest at Powers Apartments and was famous for her crab-catching ability.] "Noni let us go along sometimes over by Fort Screven. We'd put chicken necks on the lines, wade out waist deep and drop the lines until they hit bottom. Then we'd wait, which is not an easy thing to do when you're young. We'd slowly pull up our lines and scoop up the crabs and drop them in a tall bushel basket. A good crabbing day yielded two to three baskets, filled to the brim." (SLK)

"I remember watching Mama Lou drop the live crabs into pots of boiling water on the stove." (MLK)

"Louise would sit at the kitchen table, which was spread with old newspapers, and pick crabs all day. Then she would make crab stew the simple way with milk, boiled eggs, salt and pepper, and crab, of course. She'd store jars of stew in the refrigerator crammed with all kinds of stuff. My ninety-something grandmother, whom we called Ma, loved crab stew." (PPS)

"Every night we'd pop popcorn with lots of oil in a shaker pan covered with layers of folded newspaper instead of a glass lid." (SLK)

"I remember listening to Granddad's stories and watching the moon rise up over the ocean, watching to see if water dripped off it like he told us." (SLK)

First published in 2005 in the Morning News.

Tybee II:
Time Spent at the Pavilion

Lucile Wilson Jackson moved to Tybee in 1936 when she was thirteen. "My father built the Wilson Hotel on 16th Street, where we lived," she recalled. She soon met other teenagers, including her husband-to-be, Ralph Jackson.

She continued: "I remember the pavilion with the big silver ball hanging over the dance floor...I remember the Brass Rail Pavilion that had a dance floor with a juke box, where we dropped in a nickel and danced to all the famous bands' music."

Mary Butler's Restaurant was next door to the Wilson Hotel but burned down during the fire that also destroyed the pavilion, Lucile said.

Lytell S. Calhoun, eighty-five, of Metter recalled spending a month each summer at the Carbo House. "When I was about sixteen our local paper [the *Metter Advertiser*] selected me to be in a beauty contest at the pavilion," she said. "Mother bought me a fine white latex bathing suit from Fine's. I was one scared country girl."

Across from the pavilion was a big bathhouse that had bathing suits for rent. "They were all black and most of them hung to your knees," Lytell said. "I didn't rent one, but I don't imagine mine looked any better."

Freda Dzielinski equates memories of Tybee with longtime resident E.B. Izlar. "What a delightful person he was," she said. "My sister and I called him 'Uncle Earnest' because of the friendship our families had over many years."

Freda also remembers riding the train to Tybee. "We children would run to the pavilion to reserve a picnic table and rocking chairs for the grown-ups."

Freda, who is eighty-six, describes her Tybee memories as "oh, so sweet."

As a child, Sister M. Lillian Quadrella of the Religious Sisters of Mercy practically lived at the skating rink on the pier. "My dad would give me the money for renting the skates every Sunday afternoon. I was so proud when Mom and Dad bought me my own skates when I was in the seventh grade. But, they bought me a size eight. I never grew into them (I'm still a size six), but they were my pride and joy."

Old-timers remember the various Tybee pavilions. *Courtesy of the author.*

The skating rink also brought back memories for Lesellene DeLoach. "You could skate out in the awesome breeze and over the water feeling as though you could go on into eternity."

When Mary Alice Hendrix visited grandmother Thelma Lamar at Tybee, she and her cousins, Craig and Connie, would often go skating at the pier.

"I remember rounding the corner on the water side and feeling the refreshing mist of the water and trying to keep from slipping and falling on the wet wooden floor."

Andrea Guyer Padgett's parents owned Cobb's Apartments on 17th Street. "My sister and I grew up understanding what hard work was like," she said. "We had plenty of chores before the fun could start. I practically grew up at Chu's Department Store and Bill's Grill eating corn dogs and playing baseball pinball."

Jay Stewart also enjoyed Cobb's and Bill's Grill. "Some of my happiest childhood memories are from Tybee days with family while we stayed at Cobb's Apartments," he said. "I spent hours at the baseball pinball machines at Bill's Grill hoping to reach twenty-five runs, which entitled you to a stuffed dog that sat atop the pinball machines."

First published in 2005 in the Morning News.

Tybee III:
Family Memories and More

Fred Clark remembers when Tybee's 10th Street was just a dirt road. "Our house faced the ocean and had a view of it since the area between 10th Street and 10th Terrace was vacant land. Butler Avenue consisted of a one-lane oyster shell road with room to pass going in each direction. It was divided by a median that was bordered with palm trees. There was a walking path also consisting of oyster shells in the middle of the median. At a very young age I could walk across Butler Avenue without parental supervision," Clark said.

Fred began walking the beach as a teenager. "This walking habit has stayed with me," he said. "I look forward to the summer months when I can walk the beach where I am totally relaxed and energized. I thoroughly enjoy seeing people I seldom see during the year. One such venture resulted in my meeting a beautiful young woman who had just graduated from the University of South Carolina and returned to Savannah. Nancie Meddin became my wife."

Jack Boylston believes all Tybeeians fear crossing Lazaretto Creek.

"Part of that fear may have come from the old bridge," he said. "I remember as a child riding down the Tybee Road and, as you approached the bridge, there was a sign [that said] 'Cross at your own risk.' I can remember my Dad slowly entering the bridge. I watched every wooden plank we crossed in fear that the bridge would collapse. I dreaded it when it was time to go back to the mainland but the bridge made it worse."

When Lee Friedman was growing up at Tybee, his father, like other businessmen, would drive into town each morning to work and return to the island at night.

"Since this was before air conditioning, most of the Jewish people would congregate on the boardwalk next to [the pavilion] at night for the cool air and camaraderie," he recalled. Lee's father bought their Second Avenue house in 1939 for $2,500, furnished. In 1945, his uncle sold a home on the Back River for $10,000. The asking price of many Back River homes now tops $1 million.

Tybee's Butler Avenue once had a median with palm trees. *Courtesy of the Fred Garis Jr. family.*

Tina Gaudry Lales remembers her father, Bill, coming on the beach only on Sunday at high tide after church, but before golf came on the television. "However, we were just horrified because he would always wear tennis shoes to swim," she said.

Sherry Ginsberg Belford can't forget lifeguards like Aron Weiner and Sonny Seiler or her brother, Ronnie, tracking down past-due floats.

From 1950 to 1965, Renee Portman Dunn's family stayed the summer on Shirley Road between 9th and 10th Streets. "We spent a huge amount of time at the Fresh Air Home," she said. "We helped set the tables, made peanut butter sandwiches, played with cook's daughter and were even babysat by the counselors. I had a closet full of wooden crosses [given out on the last Sunday of the children's two-week visits] and learned several hymns there."

Lokey Lytjen, who now lives in Wyoming, remembers fun times with cousins, including Catherine McKenzie Bowman. One summer, they decided to build a whiskey still after Lokey's brother learned about one in school. "We got a lot of the materials from the vacant lot across from Robbie DePue's house…Mr. DePue had a conniption fit when he got home and learned of our ingenuity."

Lokey's cousin, Catherine, grew up in New Jersey, but spent part of every summer at Tybee. "My grandmother, Mama Ree [Marie McKenzie], and

Aunt Regina Lytjen had a home on 11th Street and Second Avenue," she explained. She remembers playing stickball in the street and, like many others, recalled chasing the mosquito truck on bicycles. "What were we thinking?!" she said.

Jeni Ellis-Riggs's family stayed at Cobb's Apartments and later at the McCall Cottage. "We'd sleep on the porch in the hammock or in the lounge chairs. We played games and cards at night and took walks on the beach."

Barbara J. Figg now lives in Arizona but has keen memories of childhood days at Tybee. "I lived with my Aunt Amy and Uncle Jeff Dickey. They operated a combination market, bar and restaurant, which we called 'the store,' but the sign over the door said 'Dickey's.' My cousins and I would walk barefoot from the Back River to the post office to get my aunt and uncle's mail…we would run from one shady spot to another trying to keep our feet from burning. Sometimes it was two kids holding onto each other crowding in one small round shadow of shade."

Jean Fields Holstein played tag with the twenty children of all ages who lived on 10th Street, watched half-rubber games on the beach and listened to deejay Jerry Rogers on the radio.

Memories from Mallie Clark Jr. include plywood whop boards, camping on Little Tybee and the Icehouse, his family's business. "Since those days, however, I've experienced much better memories," he said. "The memories enjoyed as a parent raising my own children on Tybee, and being an integral part of their memories, have been much better than anything that came before."

First published in 2005 in the Morning News.

Readers Reminisce About Daffin Park

Daffin Park was named for Philip Dickinson "P.D." Daffin, who was a member of the Savannah Park and Tree Commission for more than thirty years, beginning in 1896. A few years ago Robert Bennett wrote about Daffin in a detailed paper now on file at the Georgia Historical Society. Bennett's work paints an interesting and entertaining portrait of the man responsible for many of Savannah's beautiful moss-laden live oak trees.

Daffin, born in Florida in 1841, lived in Savannah most of his life. He was a cotton merchant and was involved in various community activities, but as Bennett writes, "his work on the Park and Tree Commission way overshadowed all of these [other interests]."

One of the first achievements of the Park and Tree Commission after Daffin took over was the improvement of the Colonial Cemetery. Evidently, the famous graveyard at Oglethorpe Avenue and Abercorn Street had been neglected for many years. Weeds had taken over and gravesites were in sad shape.

The commission's next project was the Oglethorpe Avenue median, which was planted with oaks from East Broad Street to West Broad Street (now Martin Luther King Boulevard).

Next the group, chaired by Daffin, turned its attention to sprucing up Emmet Park and the city's famous squares. The planting of Victory Drive's stately palmetto trees was yet another of the commission's projects.

Evidently Daffin was a colorful character who sported a snow-white beard and colorful neckties. He walked with a cane, talked with a "barking sense" and enjoyed a daily toddy, Bennett wrote.

When it came time to name what was then the new recreational park in the "southeastern part of the city," the city fathers chose to call the area Daffin Park instead of the other considered name, Davis Park (as in Jefferson). Daffin Heights subdivision and Daffin Drive also were named for him.

Daffin died in 1929 at age eighty-eight and rumor has it, according to Bennett, that the famous Savannahian, who was a widower, caught a fatal cold while looking out the window at a couple of pretty girls.

Years ago, when the development of Daffin Park was in the planning stages, the city fathers wanted it to be a "first-class recreation park…and in the course of time…one of the famous pleasure grounds in the United States." In those days, the park was on the outskirts of town. Now the area is known as midtown.

No doubt about it, Daffin Park, which was designed between 1906 and 1909, has become one of the city's most popular leisure spots. Whether it's the swimming pool, tennis courts, ball fields or lake, thousands of people harbor special memories of Daffin Park.

Annie Lou Sewell Richards, ninety-two, first visited Daffin in 1926 or 1927, just after her family moved to Savannah.

"On our first Sunday afternoon [here] my sister and I walked to Daffin Park," she recalled. "A record was playing the song, 'Who.' After that we would walk to the park many mornings in our swimsuits with a lightweight robe over them. Neighbors Frances Kent and Lovie Bailey would accompany us."

In 1968, after living away from Savannah for many years, Mrs. Richards and her husband returned to see the sights. "My husband took my picture in Daffin Park by the same shrub [that I had my picture taken in front of] when I was seventeen."

Michael Carbonell describes himself as a "lifetime member of the Daffin Park Gang."

"I am fifty-seven and have many indelible memories of my life as a young kid and teenager in the Daffin Park 'arena,'" he said. "I grew up on East 40th Street between Waters Avenue and Live Oak Street (the center of the world during the 1950s and '60s)."

"Daffin Park was a huge, safe, baby-sitting playground," he said. "Our parents had a certain comfort level and just turned us loose."

Michael started playing tennis at Daffin Park when he was twelve. "The tennis facility was and still is awesome." In those days, Michael borrowed a racket until he saved up for one.

"My mother gave me her weekly accumulation of S&H Green Stamps for my chores. I saved enough but it took forever (ten full books). I was so cool with my Poncho Gonzales racket. It was all wood and came with a screw-down form to prevent warping. Twenty-five or so rackets later I still enjoy tennis, thanks to Daffin."

Amanda McLaughlin Cannon, who grew up in the 500 block of East 49th Street and in the 600 block of East 44th Street, also fits the "Daffin Park neighborhood profile."

"From the time I was about in the third grade I remember going to the pool at Daffin with my neighborhood friends, Patty and Tommy Daniels, Judy and Ann Nash and my brother, Robert McLaughlin. Often we went twice per day, going home for lunch and returning for the afternoon session. In the months when the pool was closed, we fished, rode bikes or played on the playground."

Amanda also was a Panthers football cheerleader. "Our practices were at Daffin so I walked over every day after school but I had to be home by dark. I remember an end-of-the-season 'bowl day' at Grayson Stadium when I was sponsored by a team captain and got to walk out on the field before the game with a huge mum bouquet just like they did at the BC [Savannah] High School game."

By the time Amanda was in junior high, she and her friends walked to the park to watch BC practice football. "In high school Daffin Park activity switched to watching baseball games or gathering across from the Triple X restaurant to hang out or make plans."

When Amanda married Tommy Cannon, they lived in an apartment across Victory Drive from Ambuc Stadium for two years. "My three daughters attended Blessed Sacrament School and had recess in Daffin Park everyday. [In September] my granddaughter celebrated her second birthday with a party at the Daffin Park playground."

First published in 2005 in the Morning News.

Daffin Park II:
Fishing and Bonfires

For many folks, Daffin Park conjures up memories of fishing as well as the annual bonfires.

Chuck Courtenay, who now lives near Augusta, remembers going to the park with his grandfather, "Pop" Ubele. "As I got older I would fish in the pond behind the pool with my friends," Chuck said. "We would bring pieces of biscuit dough for bait. The fish were not very big but we did not care. Just the excitement of catching fish was enough for us."

Whenever Chuck comes home to Savannah, Daffin Park is always on his list of places to visit and reminisce.

John Carbonell's "best discovery" at Daffin was the pond, "especially since I was nature boy, son of Tarzan, who could live off the island" in the middle. It didn't take long for John to master the art of bamboo cane pole fishing. "With a can of fresh alley worms, I could always return home with a string full of four-inch bream, which I delighted in feeding to the jungle cats that lived in the dark alley behind our house on East 40th Street."

Eventually John saved enough money from returning empty soda bottles and washing a neighbor's new 1953 Oldsmobile to buy a "shiny, new closed face Zebco 33 spinning reel and glass rod at Jimmy Carr's Sporting Goods Shop on Waters Avenue."

Unfortunately every other cast was a struggle for John, who reeled in pounds of green slime. One day the pond was nearly drained and all he could see was slime. No giant bass could possibly live there. "It was like a bad dream and it stunk to high heaven," he recalled. "[It was] my first case of depression."

Michael Hennessy remembers the bonfire in Daffin greeting the New Year. After bonfires were banned in the downtown squares, they moved to Daffin.

"Around the middle of December, the city would send a bulldozer to the area of Daffin that adjoined Grayson Stadium," he said. The dozer would dig out a circle thirty to forty feet in diameter and this would become the site of the bonfire.

The Daffin Park bonfires always were a popular event. *Courtesy of the* Savannah Morning News.

"Once school let out for the holidays, the site would swarm with neighborhood boys," he added. "As I remember it, the Bazemore brothers, Gary and Larry, were in charge. Others working on the fire included Calvin Seckinger, Tommy Hogan, Billy Adams and Joe Counihan. Someone loaned us a dump truck and we would ride around Savannah collecting old boxes, tires, outhouses, small boats and once even a coffin from Albert Goette's funeral home."

After Christmas Michael and the boys would collect unsold Christmas trees from the lots and add them to the pile. Also, nearby residents would bring their trees to the park. On the morning of December 26, the frame—four tree trunks—would be erected within the circle. "The poles were twenty-five to thirty feet tall and would be set in a rectangle about twelve feet on each side," he explained.

Once the poles were erected, the building began. Crude sides made of two-by-fours were attached to the poles and the tires, boxes and trees were piled up. "As the pile grew, more sides were constructed until the pyre was thirty feet high."

"By New Year's Eve there was furious activity to finish up," he continued. "About dark on the 31st, the pile was doused with kerosene. It was considered an honor to be chosen to climb the pyre with a can of the stuff to pour on it. As midnight approached, the crowd would gather. To a young Savannah teenager it seemed like everyone in Savannah was there. In reality, it was probably around four thousand. At midnight a torch would be lighted and flung upon the bonfire. It would ignite the pyre and, to the accompaniment of firecrackers, the New Year would be welcomed."

Michael and others said the bonfires were discontinued when a spectator was injured from fireworks shot off in the crowd.

First published in 2005 in the Morning News.

Daffin Park III:
Swimming in the Pond and Pool

Shirley Jones Marks and countless others learned to swim at the old Daffin Park pool next to the pond, which was shaped like a map of the United States.

"I remember the bottom of the pool was nothing but mud," Shirley said.

One of Shirley's earliest memories was the time the pond froze—probably in the mid-1930s—and her father (Earl P. Jones) let her walk on the ice, while he stood on terra firma holding tightly to her hand.

Kit Chandler Pelletreau also remembers the original pool and sketched a map of it in a note she wrote to me.

"A low concrete wall separated the boating area from the swimming areas," she explained. A wooden boardwalk was between the shallow and deep ends where stationary floats offered endless fun.

"Admission to swimming was five cents," she added. "We didn't always have [the money] and could sneak in by wetting ourselves in the boating waters behind the bathhouses and rush into the pool as if we'd already been swimming.

"The pool opened early—how cool and fresh—and we could spend the whole day into the evening hours…lifeguards strictly forbade our going on the deep side until we earned a swimmer's button by swimming half the length of the pool—about fifty yards."

Kit and her friends had to be home when parents got in from work (if they had jobs), she said. "If you lived in the Old Fort [downtown] it was a long walk. Starved after a day in the water, we raided the fruit trees in backyards along the way—especially from the lane in back of Victory Drive homes."

All her life Kit says she has "thanked the city fathers who built that huge complex (called Daffin Park). "In the Depression we kids would've sweltered without its cooling waters in the summer. Even on cold days we went there to catch minnows."

Rebekah L. Saunders and her older sisters rented bathing suits for a dime. "We looked forward to summer and frequent trips to Daffin," she

The old Daffin Park pool had a sandy bottom. *Courtesy of the Fred Garis Jr. Family.*

said. "I learned to swim there and almost learned to dive. Once I swam over to the island that had the weeping willow trees (we weren't supposed to go to the island)."

Around 1954 a new L-shaped swimming pool was built at Daffin. Michael Hennessey remembers watching his cousin, Dallas McClellan, adjusting the pool lights for Thomas and Hutton Engineering.

When the pool opened, Fred Lindsay was water safety director for the American Red Cross, which offered swimming lessons at the pool. Once you became a "beginner" swimmer there were "intermediate" and "swimmer" classes to master, as well as rowing and motor boating offered in the pond by Kenny Medernack, he said.

By age eight Michael had passed all the classes and began working with the volunteers. "I hesitate to start recalling names because I know I will leave someone out but among those were Mrs. Quante, Mrs. Shearouse, Mary Johnson, Mary Barton, Edith Walker and Larry Bacon. Among the other teachers were Dan, Kit and Tom Parker, Jinny and Kirk Johnson, Alice and Arlene Quante, Del Little, Laurie Jenkins, Jane Hammick, Scotty and Angela Paul, William Sidney Jarrell, Priscilla Shearouse, Noni Barton and my brother Terence.

"All the people mentioned above are north of fifty," he said. "Some are long dead. None are forgotten."

Susan Rahal Graebener was another who took swimming lessons at Daffin in the late '50s. "I can still remember the strong smell of chlorine water, the overhead spray that we had to walk through before entering the pool at the turnstile with the wooden floor and the zillion kids and their different stations around the pool with instructors and cheering parents behind the metal fence trying to get a glimpse of their star child or children."

First published in 2005 in the Morning News.

Daffin Park IV:
Grayson Stadium and Endless Fun

From 1955 to 1989, Randy Brannen and his family lived on Victory Drive just across the street from Daffin Park. He and his siblings have hundreds of memories about Daffin, including playing at Grayson Stadium.

"We would climb up onto the wall in the back where it wasn't too high," Randy said. "One game we played was to walk all the way around the stadium without touching the ground. It makes me cringe to think about this now, but when we got to the east side of the enclosed part of the stadium near third base, we would climb up the side of the structure by using the bricks that stuck out irregularly. Imagine your ten-year-old climbing up the side of a two-story building like this."

His brother, Bill, remembers hearing that Mickey Mantle and the New York Yankees were playing an exhibition game at the stadium. Their sister Diane went to watch with their father.

Emory Bazemore lived on West Duffy Street in the 1930s and '40s and often walked to Daffin.

"It cost twenty-five cents to see the Savannah Indians as a member of [Judge Victor Jenkins's] Knothole Club," he recalled. "The boys who lived in my neighborhood earned money by selling peanuts or shining shoes in the 'big park' [Forsyth] or carrying bags of groceries home for ladies who shopped at the Big Star on Henry Street."

As a child Michael Hennessy walked with his father, brother and sister to the Daffin playground. "After swinging and playing on the merry-go-round we would go to Mr. Neimeyer's store on Waters and Washington Avenue lane for a soda."

Michael also remembers Santa Claus landing in a small plane in the park. "He would get into a convertible and throw bubblegum to us as he left for Adler's Department Store downtown."

John Carbonell also lived a few blocks away from the park.

"The park was Grayson Stadium and the opportunity to watch the Savannah Indians play real baseball, not the half rubber we played on 40th Street with a broom handle."

Bobby Adams recalled how his brother and their next-door neighbor set fire to the park. "It seems that these youngsters dug a foxhole in the park so they could play army," he said. One day one of the boys found a book of matches to play with and set the grass on fire. "It got so big that someone had to call the fire department to put out the blaze.

"Oh, by the way," Bobby continued, "they picked Thanksgiving Day to set the park on fire, right in the middle of the BC-Savannah High Thanksgiving Day football game. Fans were standing up and looking over the rails in the right field bleachers to see how close the flames would come to the cars."

Robbie Collins's grandfather, L.J. Harris, leased the public address systems to the City of Savannah at both Grayson and Ambuc stadiums. "My older brother Randy and I spent many a game in the dugout at Grayson," he said. "Occasionally we were allowed to work the scoreboard lights or attend a wrestling match featuring Sputnik Monroe."

Charles Skinner remembers running across the park at night with Walter Thomas after a baseball game at Grayson Stadium baseball. "We were pretty young and it was dark," he said.

One Sunday afternoon Charles's late brother, John, scrambled for a foul ball at Grayson and fell down, skinning his knees just to get a ball for his little brother.

"I still have that baseball," Charles said.

In the late 1930s, Herbie Griffin and several other Benedictine boys formed a baseball team called the Shamrocks. "All of us still living in Savannah (including Jack White and Sonny Joyce) remember the old park and skating rink…Fred Garis's Tiger Club practiced in the afternoon and BC bused the football players to Daffin to practice."

Larry Homansky moved to Savannah from New York and made plenty of friends at Daffin Park. "I would go skating [at the rink] next to the pool," he said. "On a summer day or on the weekend, it was a great place to meet new people and have a great time."

John C. McCarthy III says he shudders to think what his life would have been like without Daffin Park.

"My first paying job was selling Christmas trees for the Italian Club," he said. "Mr. Al Orsini helped every kid who worked there and there was none finer than Mr. Al." John's summer job at Grayson Stadium involved sitting on the roof to retrieve foul balls. "It was the best seat in the house but that was before lawyers," he said.

"Daffin Park was life and we lived it," he added. "It was safe and there was always something to do. I walked or rode my bike everywhere." Once he fell off his bicycle when the chain came off and a worker from the Kiddie Fair fixed it "before I could get back up."

He remembers seeing local baseball standouts like Frankie Harper hit a baseball into Washington Avenue and Joe Herb knock a homerun out of Grayson Stadium.

"The memories are priceless and I cherish them," he said.

First published in 2005 in the Morning News.

I first wrote about Daffin Park in 1991 in the Savannah Evening Press *after Savannah's Downtown Rotary Club led the way in beautifying the pond. Members of other rotary clubs and other concerned citizens also helped with the effort, which had a goal of $125,000 in improvements. In 2005 I wrote other columns for the* Morning News *asking readers to send in their thoughts about Daffin in anticipation of the park's 2007 centennial celebration.*

Group Paying Tribute to Eastside Neighborhood

Between 1942 and 1945, the Southeastern Shipbuilding Corporation in Savannah built eighty-eight Liberty ships, including the SS *James Oglethorpe*, which met its demise when it was torpedoed by a German U-boat.

Most shipyard workers lived in Pine Gardens and in a handful of other eastside neighborhoods created during World War II to house workers at Southeastern and two additional shipbuilding firms.

Like many Baby Boomers, Charles Varner grew up in Pine Gardens, where he cultivated lifelong friendships. Now he and several pals hope to pay tribute to their former neighborhood by nominating it to the National Register of Historic Districts. Charles, along with Patricia Lennox Jenkins, Dolly Jeffers and Daisy Riner Harrison are working diligently to add their former stomping grounds to the National Register.

Pine Gardens, along with Tattnall Homes, Deptford Place and Moses Rogers Grove, were modest homes and apartments in the vicinity of President Street and Pennsylvania Avenue in close proximity to the Savannah River. The houses in these areas were "not large or particularly elegant" but good examples of homes used by the working class during and after World War II, Charles said. It's interesting to note that 750 houses in Tattnall Homes, for example, were built in just five months to accommodate the shipyard workers. The homes were named for Navy Commander Josiah Tattnall who coined the phrase, "blood is thicker than water."

Pine Gardens is the only neighborhood that remains intact and, for that reason among others, Charles believes it will make an excellent candidate for the National Register.

Charles also created a Savannah memories group at yahoo.com where he and others share memories of years gone by. (To find this site, go to yahoo.com, find groups and type in "Savannah memories.")

Herb Hilderbrand described Pine Gardens as a "great place" to grow up. "There were lots of stores to ride your bike to and you could always ride or walk down to Causton Bluff at the river…we had no color televisions,

The Union Mission once held church services at the Deptford Homes Administration Building. *Courtesy of Larry Usry.*

computers and video games in those days. No cell phones either. What a great way to live…"

Other messages posted on the site discuss the various neighborhood stores, including Prince and Miller's Grocery. One person recalls buying RC in a bottle and candy called Squirrel Nuts from an establishment called Mitchell's.

First published in 2005 in the Morning News.

Joe Tilton Treasures Happy Days on Wilmington Island

If you drive all the way to the end of Wilmington Island Road, past dozens of riverfront homes, around the sharp "S" curve and the big oak tree in the middle of the road, you'll find yourself smack dab in Joe Tilton's front yard.

Joe and his wife, Freddie, live on what is known as the south end of the island—a quiet, serene area overlooking Sheepshead Creek and, in the distance, Wassaw Sound. The Tilton family's ties to Wilmington go way back, long before there were places like Wilmington Park or Bull River Plantation and years before traffic-clogged highways wound their way to the island.

Tilton's great-grandfather, Civil War hero Major Nathaniel O. Tilton, spent summers on Wilmington. Nathaniel's obituary noted that when Union forces were closing in on Tybee Island, he volunteered to take the Confederate batteries out of harm's way to Savannah. Joe has the handwritten deed, dated 1892, showing that some of his ancestors' property was purchased by the Wilmington Island Pleasure and Improvement Co.

Tilton's parents bought their waterfront lots in the 1920s from Henry Walthour for what would now be a pittance. They built a dock house they called "Happy Days," which was destroyed in the 1947 hurricane. That was after many happy days of crabbing and shrimping on the banks of Sheepshead Creek.

The thousands of people who live in subdivisions, condominiums and apartments (with all the modern conveniences) probably can't imagine what it was like growing up in Joe Tilton's day when only a handful of residents called the island home.

Not that those days were the dark ages or anything, but in the 1930s and '40s, Wilmington was like Daufuskie Island, South Carolina, before development began. Four or five oyster factories dotted the huge wooded island. And before the road to the island was built, folks came by canoe from Thunderbolt.

Joe Tilton remembers happy days growing up on Wilmington Island. *Courtesy of Joe Tilton.*

During an impromptu tour of Wilmington, Joe told plenty of funny stories while pointing out some of his old haunts.

"This is how the roads were when I was a kid," he said as we bounced along a bumpy dirt stretch. We wound our way back to Wilmington Island Road, a stone's throw away from what was once the Walthour Golf Course (there were two golf courses on the island then).

"When the golf course was abandoned, we got permission to hunt squirrels along what used to be the fairways," Joe recalled. "Wilmington Park was pure old woods then."

Lest we not forget Willie Young's garden on the south end of the island. Willie grew fruits and vegetables and carried them to the other side of the island to his produce stand, a small, mustard-colored building that still stands at the intersection of Wilmington Island and Cromwell Roads.

Joe and buddies like Harold McCarthy had a fondness for Willie's watermelons. One day, the boys got a tip that Willie would be at church on Sunday night. They figured that might be a good time for them to "borrow" a few of the sweet, juicy melons.

"It took us about twenty minutes to climb the fence," Joe said. Finally, the young raiders made it over the fence and headed for the melons. Suddenly a figure wielding a shotgun emerged from the woods. One shotgun blast later, Joe and friends were off, lickety-split.

"We took that fence in one leap," he said. They never knew for sure who put an end to their plan.

The memories continued to pour out as Joe drove past the site of a huge turkey farm, Liberty Hall Plantation, the Meldrim property, Green's Fishing Camp and Pittman's Tavern, Cabin Camp and South Wind. Except for the General Oglethorpe Hotel and the golf course, that was just about it for Wilmington back then.

First published in 1988 in the Evening Press.

Can You Go Home Again?
These Folks Did

A couple of months ago when Helen Cranman's sister was in town for the funeral of their 101-year-old mother, they rode by their childhood home.

"The woman who lives there was in the front yard so we stopped and talked," Helen said. Before the two sisters knew it they were taking an impromptu tour of the home their father built in 1924.

"My father [Joseph Schmalheiser] built the house at 524 East 45th Street. In 1924, the year before I was born," said Helen, who remembered how her father put together a radio and placed it in the built-in shelves in the dining room.

All these years later, Helen can still remember the names of many of the families who lived on the block: Exley, Byck, Middleton, Keating and Minis, among others.

The Schmalheisers lived on 45th Street until 1943, when they moved to California. Helen's father worked with his brother, Edward, in the movie business.

Helen relayed her story to me after she read last week's column about people visiting their former homes. Can you go home again?

Like many folks, Jane Kahn says it's difficult to go back to any of the places—"my homes or my parents' or grandparents'"—that were filled with wonderful memories.

"My grandparents lived in Ardsley Park (the official one, not the fringe)," she said. Several years ago, Jane went to a Realtor's open house at her grandparents' former home. She was taken aback when she discovered that the owners had decorated the home with country pieces and accessories, unlike the formal furniture that she was accustomed to seeing in the house when her grandparents lived there.

Jane told the Realtor the history of her grandfather having been the real Miss Daisy's brother and the visits her Aunt Lena Fox and her chauffeur, Will, made to the house through the years.

"Last month, Aunt Lena's granddaughter, Ann Uhry Abrams [the *Driving Miss Daisy* playwright's sister] was visiting me from Atlanta," she said. "We drove by the home and the current owner…was outside. We stopped and she graciously invited us in, but sadly we didn't have time."

Whenever Marge Hester leaves her serene riverfront refuge in Bluffton, South Carolina, for a trip to Savannah, she often drives by the East 46th Street house that she and her family called home for more than thirty years. "I take a tour down 46th Street," Marge admitted.

Even though she and her late husband, Dr. Bob Hester, sold the house a dozen years ago, Marge still enjoys seeing her old home with its abundance of azaleas and shrubbery.

In fact, when the house was for sale, Marge, Suzanne Tippett (her daughter) and the former Hester Tippett (her granddaughter) were able to sneak a peek inside when a Realtor hosted an open house.

"It was delightful, especially for my granddaughter, Hester, who fell in love with it all over again," she said. "We were well pleased with the improvements."

The house, which overlooks Kavanugh Park, was built in 1912 by George Heyward. It was constructed in a style that resembled houses in Maine, which was where Mrs. Heyward lived as a child. The Heywards moved from 46th Street around 1930. Former residents also include the Calhoun family.

For some folks, going through their former homes brings back a flood of warm memories of days gone by. They can close their eyes and recall miniscule details that often conjure up a great deal of nostalgia.

Beth Lattimore Reiter's former home on Washington Avenue has the distinction of being the first house built in Ardsley Park. The spectacular structure at the corner of Washington Avenue and Abercorn Street was completed in 1910. Present owners James and Lee Ann Holcomb spent four years refurbishing the house.

Beth had the opportunity to go through the home that her grandfather built when renovation was being done. She said that she is thrilled with the work.

Thomas Wolfe said you can't go home again, but some people can.

First published in 2004 in the Morning News.

Exploring Isle of Hope's Wymberley

When James Richmond developed Isle of Hope's Wymberley subdivision in 1946, the trees and underbrush were so dense the heavy equipment operators had a tough time breaking ground.

"It was so wild we couldn't even get a bulldozer in there," he recalled. Finally, the developer decided to burn the foliage, a move that resulted in a "terrific fire," he said.

Richmond purchased the 150 acres from Bill Flinn, who operated a sawmill in the area. It was Richmond's first "personal" development and he undertook the venture with "great fear and trepidation."

He called the subdivision Wymberley after the eldest son of Noble Jones, the colonial Georgian who made his home at nearby Wormsloe Plantation.

Richmond named one of his daughters Wymberley and dubbed many of the streets in the subdivision after family members: Richmond Drive, Diana Drive and Nancy Drive (for other daughters). Flinn Drive was named for Bill Flinn and Avenue of Pines was something Richmond "just came up with."

During the 1940s Richmond sold many of the houses he built at Wymberley for $8,000.

After finishing Wymberley, Richmond developed several smaller subdivisions throughout Savannah and built a couple of noteworthy homes, including the white brick house on the northeast corner of Washington Avenue and Habersham Street and the two-story house with the curved staircase on Victory Drive between Paulsen and Harmon Streets.

In the early 1950s, Richmond established Fairway Oaks at Waters and DeRenne Avenues, which proved to be quite an adventure.

"I never dealt with so many snakes in my life," Richmond said, adding that one day he accompanied the bulldozer operator out to the land that would become Fairway Oaks. The bulldozer was knocking down trees when "Mr. Pound from Pound's Dairy" came over and asked him to push over a dead tree.

When the tree went down, about one hundred chicken snakes slithered out from the debris. The bulldozer squished the reptiles, but Richmond said seeing all those snakes "upset me so much I left and didn't go back that day."

A Laurel, Mississippi, native, Richmond came to Savannah by way of New York City and Columbia University, where he studied playwriting. He ended up being the manager of the Plaza Theatre in New York because "being a Southerner, I knew how to run it."

Richmond met his future wife, who was from Savannah, when his sister made her debut in New York. "I was supposed to be watching out for my sister, but I was watching my wife, instead," he said.

Richmond's father-in-law was the chairman of the board of the S&A Railroad and "ran the town of Port Wentworth," he said. Richmond came to Port Wentworth to develop 150 homes for workers at a new shipyard that was to be built in the Westside community.

When the war was over, Richmond decided to stay because he "loved Savannah."

First published in 1989 in the Morning News.

LePageville Lives Again in Church Painting

Cyndy Blount is an artist who was intrigued by the story of the lost community of LePageville. She had seen a tattered black-and-white photograph of the old LePageville Baptist Church, which was demolished in the late 1960s, and knew that the congregation had moved to a building at Park and Waters Avenues. She also heard that part of the wood from the original church was used to remodel the new church, which is called St. Thomas Missionary Baptist.

The touching story tugged at Cyndy's heartstrings. As a result she was inspired to paint a picture of the old LePageville church to give to the St. Thomas congregation.

Church member Minnie Lou Robinson, eighty-two, was only twelve when she moved from LePageville into town, but the lost neighborhood remains close to her heart. She has plenty of memories of life there and, more importantly, her mother, Bessie Bowman Robinson, is buried in the cemetery.

Minnie Lou remembers walking to the Deptford Tract near the Savannah River as a girl and picking plums from an orchard. Drinking "nice, cool water" from a pump near the LePageville Church also was part of daily life.

LePageville was a black neighborhood sandwiched between what is now President Street and the Savannah River. The rows of tiny frame homes stretched from what was then Southern States Phosphate and Fertilizer Co. to just east of Pennsylvania Avenue.

Residents of nearby Pine Gardens, a tightly knit white neighborhood, also were aware of the little community known as LePageville. One of those was Patricia Jenkins, who grew up in Riverside Gardens and Deptford Homes. But she, like others, never realized a cemetery existed.

The village, as Minnie Lou describes LePageville, was organized in the late 1890s when the railroad built homes there for its workers, one of whom was her grandfather, who moved to Savannah from Orangeburg, South Carolina. Later, the neighborhood housed employees at both the Southeastern Shipbuilding Corp. and Southern States, Minnie Lou said.

Many LePageville residents worked at the nearby shipyard. *Courtesy of the Juliette Gordon Low Birthplace.*

However, as larger industries began moving into the area and buying up parcels of land, folks moved out and LePageville gradually disappeared.

As the neighborhood declined and houses were torn down, Reed Dulany Jr. of Southern States deeded the church building to the residents. After "praying out of their souls," according to church history, the deacons decided that moving the building would be cost prohibitive and the church was demolished. The congregation acquired a building on Park Avenue and changed the name to St. Thomas Missionary Baptist Church after a beloved deacon.

All this was news to Patricia Jenkins until a few years ago when her late husband, Jimmy, began clearing some of the land for a softball field.

Serendipitously, a church member saw what was happening and told them about the cemetery, which had become overgrown and choked with weeds and underbrush. Pat began working with church members like George and Jesse Ponder to help reclaim the area for the descendants of LePageville residents.

Patricia doesn't consider herself a heroine; she was "just doing what I felt like needed to be done," she explained.

As a result of Patricia's hard work, the Englehard Corp., which ended up owning the property, deeded over 3.8 acres of land to the LePageville Memorial Cemetery Corp. Alderman Ellis Cook became involved in the project, as did former Pine Gardens residents Charles Varner, David Blount and others who regularly clean up the area.

Sadly, only one gravestone remains in the cemetery. Back in the day when folks were buried there, they couldn't afford traditional headstones, Minnie Lou said. Instead, families placed whatever they could on the grave, whether it was a pitcher, a pot or even a hubcap.

First published in 2006 in the Morning News.

Midtown Area Was Formerly
Polo Grounds

If you thought polo was a sport for the rich and famous, think again. In the 1920s, when times were tough, a handful of Savannahians rode polo ponies where midtown homes sit today.

Carroll Zealy, ninety-two, of Tybee Island was one of those polo players. "We were not rich people," insists Zealy. "Back then it wasn't a popular sport because very few people knew much about it."

So how did polo end up in Savannah?

"Originally polo started with the Georgia Hussars and the Georgia National Guard's 118th Field Artillery [of which he was a member]," Zealy said. "They played until 1926 or 1927 and disbanded," he added.

A few years later, the fellows in the 118th were back at it again. Zealy joined the Guard because he was paid one dollar to go to drill on Monday nights, he said. He started playing polo in 1928.

The Guard's 118th was a cavalry unit with about one hundred horses. The majority were big draft horses that pulled guns during the annual Memorial Day parade, Zealy said. It only seemed practical that the horses be used for something else, he added. If one or two horses died, the government wouldn't replace them because of the expense of transporting them from out West.

In those days, private individuals could sell their horses to the government for one dollar in exchange for food and board. "Oats weren't cheap," Zealy said. The government only used the horses for weekly meetings and a parade or two.

A group of men decided the horses would be perfect for polo. "We had the horses, so what were we going to do?" Zealy asked.

Growing up, the boys around town had played a game called shinny, which was akin to hockey on roller skates, explained Zealy's pal, Frank Cullum. Added Zealy, "The only difference between hockey and polo is that you're short a horse in hockey."

On Sunday afternoons during the winter, cars would make their way south along Waters Avenue—in those days an oyster shell road—and make

The polo grounds were where the Olin Heights neighborhood is now. *Courtesy of the author.*

right turns into the polo field around East 54th Street. The field, which was 300 yards long and 160 yards wide, stretched down to around 63rd Street, Zealy said. "I always heard the land belonged to Dr. Barrow, who let us use it," Zealy said.

The energetic young men cleared weeds and brush from the property, planted grass and built a fence. The only building on the property was a tack house where supplies were stored. Admission was twenty-five cents a car. The vehicles would stream into the polo field and form a circle so spectators could watch the action.

Financial backers of the group included Malcolm Bell, Major Karow and Charlie Maclean, "one of the best-dressed men in Savannah," Zealy said. The All Joy Bridge Club, whose members included Addie Coleman and Mildred Cooper, held card parties to help the men raise money for grass seed.

Cullum lived on East 41st and Harmon Streets and remembers watching the horses being led down Harmon to the polo field. The animals were kept at the Atlantic Coastline Railroad facilities at Gwinnett Street and Atlantic Avenue.

"My buddy Jack Mulligan and I would fall in between the horses," Cullum recalled.

Other than Zealy, players included the likes of Bubba Coleman, Roscoe Harper, Al Watkins, Peggy McGraph and Monk Morris. The team played the University of Georgia team in Savannah and traveled to places like Augusta and Atlanta to compete. Zealy still has a silver cup that he won in a 1930 polo match.

The game was rigorous for both players and horses. "We needed four horses per person," Zealy recalled. Before Zealy began playing a man was killed when a horse fell on him. "The horse kicked him in the head," Zealy said. "If a horse falls on you, you don't wiggle. You stay still."

Mechanization of the Guard in 1934 brought an end to polo. "We didn't have free stables any more," Zealy said.

First published in 2002 in the Morning News.

Old Fort Neighborhood Rekindles Warm Memories

Ramon Alonso, ninety-two, is a quiet gentleman who smiles frequently when he recalls his days in the Old Fort section of downtown Savannah. The Alonso family, of Spanish descent, moved here from Ybor City, Florida, when eldest son Ramon was just ten.

Alonso remembers arriving at Union Station, a majestic building that stood at West Broad and Taylor Streets.

"I wish they had kept that building," Alonso said of the train station that stood in the way of Interstate 16 and what some considered progress. "My father met us and put us on the streetcar that went along Bay Street to Habersham [to their house at 410 East Bryan Street]."

From there they were scooped up and taken to the Cathedral of St. John and registered in the Marist Brothers school. "I can say that the Marist Brothers did a wonderful job," he recalled.

Alonso was one of five children in a very poor family. The house they rented on Bryan Street was in the midst of a kind of wonderland inhabited by mostly Irish families. The boys played ball and threw rocks in the nearby squares. During the holidays they went all over town collecting cardboard boxes that were piled high in Washington Square for the much-anticipated New Year's Eve bonfire.

"Eventually [the bonfires] were cut out because they became too dangerous," he said. "Some people who lived around the square had to paint their houses yearly because the heat from the fire scorched the paint."

Alonso has vivid recollections of his days in the neighborhood. "There was a cigar factory at the corner of Abercorn and Bryan Streets," he said. Going east along Bryan he remembers two Irish girls but apologizes for not being able to recall their names. A gossipy newspaper called the *Hawkeye* was in one building but "people didn't think too much of it."

The Cain, Ramsey and Gallintini families stand out in his memory. "Gallintini was a fisherman and he had a little boy who drowned at Thunderbolt," he said. Nice brick homes stood where the parking garage is on Warren Square.

Union Station was demolished to make way for the Interstate 16 ramp. *Courtesy of the Savannah Morning News.*

He also remembers families with names like Howard, Cannon, Simmons, Pelli and Dyar and a fellow called Desmond O'Driscoll.

"Slocum was a city detective," he said. "His wife was huge and when she died they had to make a special coffin."

He certainly can't forget the Rossiters. "One thing I regret is not asking Frank [Rossiter] to write a book about the Old Fort because he knew it in and out," Alonso said.

The Coca-Cola bottling plant took up the entire block running from Houston to East Broad Streets. Alonso remembers walking past the windows and watching the Coke bottles moving along the conveyor belts.

The Alonsos lived on Bryan Street until about 1920. "There were no screens on the windows and the mosquitoes were terrible," he said. They moved to Duffy Street and later to 31st Street.

Alonso worked as a printer for Union Bag for twenty-seven years. "Union Bag built this city," he said. Later he helped various local printers and was devoted to the Blessed Sacrament parish.

First published in 2001 in the Morning News.

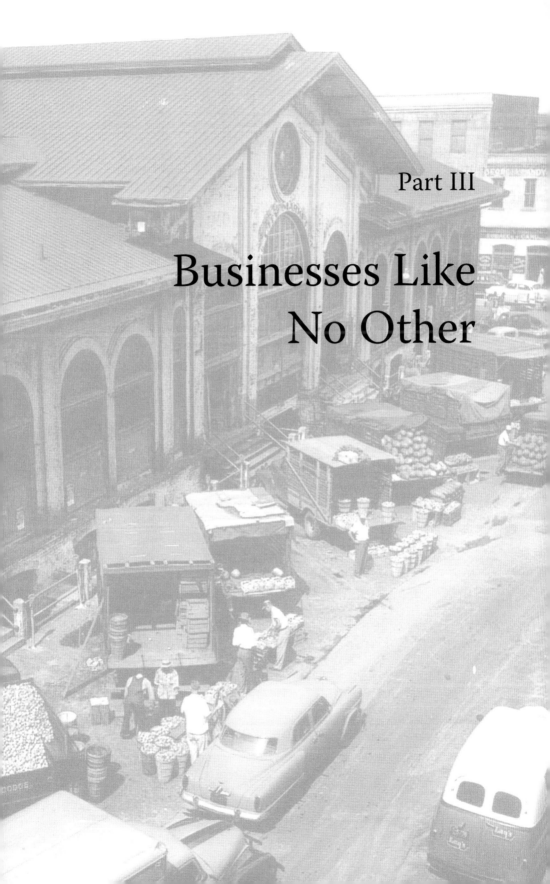

Part III

Businesses Like
No Other

Closing of Kmart on Victory Drive Brings Back Memories

Daphne Chestnut remembers the submarine sandwiches, the sliced ham and the rotating salted nuts just inside the front door at Kmart on Victory Drive. She can picture that long-gone deli counter and nearly every inch of that store like the back of her hand because she worked for the giant discount store for twenty-eight years.

On a personal note, my first summer job was in the early 1970s behind the jewelry counter at Kmart. I sold diamond rings and stored them in a safe at night, put on watchbands and punched the keys on a cash register that seemed like a dinosaur compared to today's computer versions.

Now the store is closing, which Daphne figures was coming for a while. The store's founder, S.S. Kresge, was keen on making the customer happy, a philosophy that somehow went by the wayside, Daphne said. Also, competition became fierce when more discount stores began opening, a factor that contributed to the demise of the once-popular store.

"I know that when the business isn't there you have to be realistic about stores that are not pulling their weight," she said.

But in 1963, when Kmart opened in Savannah, there were no malls and no other stores of similar size and offerings. The only other store that could compare to Kmart was Webster's off Pennsylvania Avenue, which closed in December 1962, "just before we [Kmart] opened," she said.

Daphne remembers great excitement surrounding Kmart's grand opening. A helicopter flew over the parking lot and dropped ping-pong balls, some of which contained slips redeemable for prizes.

The store that was built on top of a swamp also had its share of drainage problems through the years. "One time, during a spring tide, we had a lot of rain and the entire parking lot flooded. We had to sandbag the front door but water seeped in anyway," she recalled.

In those days the area around Victory Drive and Skidaway Road was thriving. "That corner was active," Daphne said. Larry's Restaurant was across from where Tom's is today, and Adler's, Belk's and Hancock's and other popular stores were in the shopping centers. "It was bustling," she said.

Despite its drop in popularity in recent years, Kmart on Victory Drive managed to have a "forty-year run," she added. "It really held its place for all those decades."

First published in 2003 in the Morning News.

Amanda at "Home" at Fine's

Every job has its ups and downs, but Amanda Sutton's occupation really takes the cake. And I don't mean the pineapple upside-down variety.

For twenty-two years, Amanda has been operating the elevator at Fine's on Broughton Street. And yes, as funny as it may sound in this modern age of punch-it-yourself glass elevators that leave your stomach on the first floor when they blast off, there is such a thing as an elevator operator. In fact, a couple of downtown businesses have old-timey elevators that are still in operation.

A native of Walterboro, South Carolina, Amanda's Savannah career began at a local dry cleaning establishment where she was a shirt folder. She then was recommended for a job at Fine's where she became a relief worker on the first floor.

Somehow or another, Amanda began training other employees to run the elevator. But, she said, after a series of turnovers, she decided to take things into her own hands and do the job herself.

Amanda has since been somewhat of a fixture in the elevator of the downtown store. Going up and down all day long might seem boring to some folks, but for Amanda "driving" the elevator means "never a dull moment." "I love it," she said, "It's my home away from home."

Amanda's job allows her to become acquainted with all kinds of folks. Once she even gave an elevator ride to actress Elizabeth Montgomery of television's *Bewitched*.

The elevator itself is quite quaint. Amanda stands in the front right corner of the elevator waiting for passengers. When a customer steps into the car, Amanda says, "Please watch your step." She usually wears a navy blue uniform with "Miss Amanda" monogrammed at the top. She also wears a man's work glove on one hand so it won't get roughed up during the day, closing the doors as much as she does.

Moving to the front left corner inside the elevator, she reaches across to close the outer door. Then she shuts the metal cage-like door inside the elevator and starts driving up and down.

Broughton Street was once a neon paradise. *Courtesy of the* Savannah Morning News.

Amanda has been described as a chief customer pulse-taker because she can tell if the members of her captive audience are satisfied or maybe a bit upset.

When members of Amanda's church come into the store and take a ride in the elevator, a few amens have been heard through the door. It's at those times that some are convinced that Amanda's elevator is going straight up to heaven.

First published in 1988 in the Evening Press.

Gernatt's Creamery Lives on for Family Members and Others

In the early 1920s, long before he opened his own creamery, the late Henry Gernatt delivered milk by bicycle. The milk came from John Harms's Oakhurst Farms, which, back then, was one of a handful of local dairies, such as Annette's and Starland, as well as others, no doubt.

Gernatt's daughter, Adele Gernatt Nielubowicz, who was born in 1922 at the old Telfair Hospital, remembers hearing the story of how her Daddy rode his bicycle to the Telfair to see his new baby and his wife and he "cried and cried" when the bike was stolen.

But times got better for Gernatt, who later opened Gernatt's Creamery at 41st and Montgomery Streets. Adele isn't sure exactly when the business opened, but in 1931, a picture of her younger brother, Paul William Gernatt, was featured in an ad that said "If you want to feel as fine as silk, drink more and more of Gernatt's milk."

Henry Gernatt's grandson, Chester "Ski" Nielubowicz, who lives in California, remembers details such as the five-foot-tall neon light in the shape of an ice cream cone that hung over the entrance to Gernatt's.

"My father, who was a machinist by trade, made Grandpa's popsicle and ice cream sandwich molds out of stainless steel," said Ski, who still has one of each mold. The popsicles looked as if they had been molded in a small Dixie cup, he said. "Blockbusters were like a Dixie Doodle" and were one-inch thick vanilla treats dipped in chocolate.

"My brothers, sisters and cousins, as we came of age, were asked to work in the family business," he added. "We learned to make change, wait on customers, dip ice cream and make hamburgers and hot dogs…I remember earning fifty cents an hour," but he added, "we learned important people skills for later in life."

Ski also recalls his grandfather always wearing a bow tie, "even when he was making the ice cream."

Adele said her father came to Savannah via New York State from the "old country" in eastern Europe. He worked for the railroad in Ohio and Pennsylvania and made his way down South.

In the early 1940s, Adele Gernatt posed in front of her father's business, Gernatt's Creamery. *Courtesy of Chester "Ski" Nielubowicz.*

Ski recalls his grandfather's establishment as being a "mom and pop" business similar to the modern-day convenience store.

Adele said her father wasn't an "educated man," but he read "a lot," and *True Detective* magazine, which he sold in the store, was one of his favorites. He played checkers with everyone who came into the store and often gave away ice cream. Nearby businesses included Ray's Meat Market, Ubele's and Gilmore's Dry Cleaning. In later years Gernatt expanded his business and opened the Igloo at York Lane and Bull Street.

During the 1940s and '50s Gernatt would load up a van with Blockbusters and popsicles and drive over to Savannah High School when classes were letting out. He sold popsicles for a nickel and ice cream sandwiches and Blockbusters for a dime.

Last February, while visiting Savannah, Ski went to a meeting of a Benedictine Military School alumni group (the BC Survivors) at Johnny Harris's Restaurant.

"I stood up and introduced myself," he said. "I mentioned Gernatt's Creamery and the [men's] eyes perked up and twinkled." Afterward, several of those in the audience came up to him and said they appreciated the walk down memory lane.

Henry died in 1967, a year and a half after the creamery closed.

First published in 2006 in the Morning News.

Mack's Five- and Ten-Cent Store Is a Fixture

You'll be amazed at what you see when you stroll down the aisles at Mack's Five- and Ten-Cent Store, which has been a fixture in Savannah for years.

The authentic dime-store bins at Mack's are overflowing with hard-to-find items like Lady Esther Face Powder, beaded hair nets, garters and a popular product called Medet, used for patching holes in pots and pans. The toy row offers jackstones, huge rubber spiders, sacks of marbles, brightly colored balls and tiny dolls. The seventy-nine-cent plastic snake is fun to wiggle even if thoughts of the real thing make you shiver.

The dime store, complete with a neon "Open" sign in the window, has been almost smack dab in the middle of the Medical Arts Shopping Center since the complex opened in 1959. Before that, Mr. and Mrs. Mack Youmans operated the original Mack's on Pennsylvania Avenue.

In recent years Mack's has been owned and operated by the Youmans's niece, Cathie VanWechel, who purchased the store from her mother, known by many people as Mrs. Mack. A former kindergarten teacher, Cathie switched careers when her mother decided to sell the store.

Cathie had taught school for seventeen years and she agonized over whether she should go into business for herself. She said the store's regular clientele breathed a collective sigh of relief when they heard that Mack's was staying in the family.

Cathie says she has continued to meet the demands of shoppers who look to Mack's for hard-to-find items. Teachers, for example, purchase inexpensive toys like ten-cent plastic whistles for their reward boxes.

Other customers—especially residents of nearby Stillwell Towers—are practically members of the family, she said. "They're pretty special to us," Cathie said, referring to senior citizens. "One lady we haven't seen in a while…we're trying to track her down."

Plenty of people pop into Mack's just for old-time's sake. "People who grew up around here come to visit when they come to town," Cathie said.

"One man came in with his little boy on his shoulders and said his father used to bring him in every day after school." Another woman brings her granddaughter in every week and buys her a two-dollar ring.

Folks who frequent Mack's know they can load up on hairbrush rollers with pink pins (ouch!), beaded hairnets or the Lady Esther Face Powder. "When I sell that [Lady Esther] I don't sell just one," Cathie said. "People buy four or five at once."

Cobbler aprons, plain white gift boxes and plain white shelf paper also are in heavy demand, Cathie said.

"This is a big turnover item," she said, holding up a pair of size fourteen panties. "People can't find these just anywhere."

Cathie orders constantly from several suppliers. As a result, she still manages to locate items like Skeeter Eater outdoor oil lamps and plastic rain bonnets.

First published in 1989 in the Evening Press.

His Great-Uncle Is
a Standout in History

On the right-hand wall beside the front counter at Flipper's Shoe Repair is a picture of a black man in an army uniform. The man in the photo is Henry Ossian Flipper, great-uncle of Festus Flipper Jr., proprietor of the shop at Waters Avenue and Waldburg Street.

In 1877, Henry Flipper became the first black graduate of the United States Military Academy at West Point. Every spring, during graduation ceremonies at West Point, an award given in Flipper's name is presented to the cadet "who demonstrates the highest qualities of leadership, self-discipline and perseverance in the face of unusual difficulties while a cadet."

A member of the Flipper family always presents the award and Festus hopes he will be the one to do the honors at this year's ceremonies.

Festus, fifty-five, has heard the story of Henry Flipper as long as he can remember. He's too young to have known Henry, who died at eighty-four in 1940, but in his shop he has a sack full of magazine and newspaper articles written about his famous relative.

"He was my grandfather's oldest brother," Festus said. Others brothers included a physician, a bishop in the AME Church, shoe repairmen and carriage trimmers. Festus's grandfather, Carl, taught shoe repair at Savannah State College for thirty-three years. Festus is a "third-generation shoe repair."

Festus knows the story of Henry, who was born in Thomasville, backward and forward. Henry's father, also named Festus, was a slave owned by Ephraim G. Ponder. Henry and his mother, Isabella, were owned by the Reverend Reuben H. Lucky. When Ponder moved from Thomasville to Atlanta, Festus gave his owner money to purchase Isabella and their son so the family could stay together.

Henry's education began on the plantation. "A Confederate captain's wife taught him his lower grades," Festus said. "Then he went to Atlanta University." Henry received his appointment to West Point from James Crawford Freeman, a Republican elected to Congress in 1872. "A senator wanted to purchase Henry's slot to West Point for $5,000 but he refused," Festus said.

After graduation, Henry was assigned to Fort Sill, Oklahoma. The first black officer in the army, he fought with the Tenth U.S. Cavalry—the Buffalo Soldiers—in battles against Indians, the Mexican Army gunrunners and smugglers.

In 1882, Henry was court-martialed on charges of embezzlement and was dishonorably discharged for "conduct unbecoming an officer and a gentleman."

Festus believes the charges were "trumped up," adding that "somebody pinned that mess on him."

Henry then began a thirty-seven-year career as a civil and mining engineer in the Southwest and Mexico. He also worked for an oil company in Venezuela before retiring in 1930 and settling in Atlanta.

In 1976, more than thirty years after his death, Henry was granted an honorary discharge. A copy of this document hangs beside his picture in Festus's shop.

A man named Ray MacColl was responsible for clearing Henry's name, Festus said. MacColl, a Valdosta State College graduate student and teacher in Brooks County, enlisted the help of then-U.S. Representatives Dawson Mathis and Andrew Young in his effort to exonerate Henry.

Festus continues to collect articles about Henry while he runs his shop. A bachelor, Festus is afraid his shoe repair business will die when he retires. "Kids these days would rather stand on the corner and sell crack" than make an honest living, he said.

First published in 1989 in the Evening Press.

Anna's Little Napoli Was a Tradition

For many Savannahians, birthdays, anniversaries, marriages and other momentous occasions were made extra special with a trip to Anna's Little Napoli on Skidaway Road just north of Victory Drive.

Although the cozy little Italian restaurant closed in the late 1990s, some people will never forget being ushered to tables bedecked in red-checkered cloths with a Chianti wine bottle used as a candleholder, covered with dripped wax, sitting in the center.

For many, those memories came rushing back when they read about the recent passing of Anna Modestino, the little Italian lady who opened the restaurant in 1959.

Sonja Canas-Held remembers stepping inside the eatery the night the doors opened. "My mother [Ruth Canas] and I were Anna's very first customers," she said. Sonja's father, Joe Canas, was a commercial shrimper in Thunderbolt and would often take fresh seafood to Anna.

"He also was a master craftsman," she added. "He made [Anna] a wooden whale that had her name on it [done in rope] that hung over the door to the restaurant's kitchen."

When the restaurant was enlarged, a painting in the back room depicted the riverfront in Thunderbolt showing a shrimp boat owned by Sonja's brother.

"We spent many family times there celebrating birthdays, anniversaries, first dates, marriages, etc.," she said. "Miss Anna would always come and sit with us and ask about the family and the food. That garlic cheese spread was the best I ever had," Sonja added.

Sister Alvin Seubott, administrator of St. Mary's Home, described Anna as a "gracious lady" who often thought of the St. Mary's children. "She was so good to us," Sister Alvin said. She would send over pizzas and sweets, and when Sister Alvin hosted a meeting or family gathering at the restaurant, "she would come in and make sure everything was OK."

Anna came to America from Naples, Italy, in 1947 after she married an American soldier. "She came through Ellis Island," said her son-in-law

Steve Pollak, husband of Anna's only child, Alice. In the 1950s she began making pizzas for a pizzeria next to the Steakhouse on Victory Drive. She decided to open her own place in 1959.

For many years, Anna's was one of only a handful of Italian restaurants in town. For many, it was the quintessential Italian eatery. It featured several small dining rooms decorated with strings of twinkling white lights, grapes and ivy. Italian music or opera selections played on the stereo while diners sat in cozy alcoves throughout the restaurant.

It was a quiet spot, great for relaxing with friends and family. I can just hear Miss Anna saying in broken English, "Thank you very much." And thanks to her from many for all those wonderful years.

First published in 2004 in the Morning News.

Farewell to a Broughton Street Business

"I gotta go," says Nina Greenholtz, owner of Kay's Dress Shop on West Broughton Street. "I'm aggravated because I like seeing all the neighbors but it [the closing] is something I have to do."

The recent death of her husband Lester clinched the decision for Nina. "That's when I decided to get out," she said. Like many downtown stalwarts, Lester, who was eighty, would have stayed in business forever because he "just loved it."

"He knew everybody and would stand out in front and speak to them," she said. Lester also was an avid book reader who kept dozens of books on shelves behind the cash register. "People would come in and he'd say, 'Here, take this book home for the weekend,'" Nina said. "He had a regular reading library in here.

"Lester had come into the store one Sunday to do the bills when he started feeling bad," Nina said. "He called me and I took him to the hospital." Lester died that day of viral pneumonia.

Lester and Nina opened Kay's nearly fifty years ago a block away from the present location. When plans were drawn for the courthouse, the couple moved their business.

Years ago the couple ignored naysayers who warned them not to work together. "It was fine and worked out good for us," Nina said. "I'm very good natured." Both she and her husband kept long hours Monday through Saturday at the store, which was a slice of a building two doors away from Jefferson Street. Gigantic letters that spell "Kay's" run across the front of the building.

And who is Kay?

"That's me," Nina said. Nina's maiden name is Kanter, and Kay is short for that. The store attracted a loyal following from as far away as Hilton Head Island and Ridgeland, South Carolina, she said.

The downtown parking situation, however, has been a detriment to retail business, especially small shops, Nina theorizes. "And now they have

The Annette's Dairy horse and wagon once "clippety clopped" on Broughton Street for a Junior League fundraiser. *Courtesy of the* Savannah Morning News.

gone up on tickets and meters," hurting businesses even more, she said. If a customer runs in for a pair of stockings, for example, and they get a parking ticket, it angers them, she said. "Next time they'd just as soon go to the mall."

Nina doesn't have any suggestions about what the city can do about parking, although she says other cities she has visited don't have nearly as many meters in the downtown area.

She is unsure about retirement plans and is a bit anxious about the future. "I've been doing this for so long," she said.

Currently the plate-glass windows at Kay's are plastered with huge signs announcing the going-out-of-business sale. Nina takes her place behind the huge old cash register and bids a fond farewell to a longtime customer. "You take care," the shopper says. "My best wishes to you."

First published in 1996 in the Evening Press.

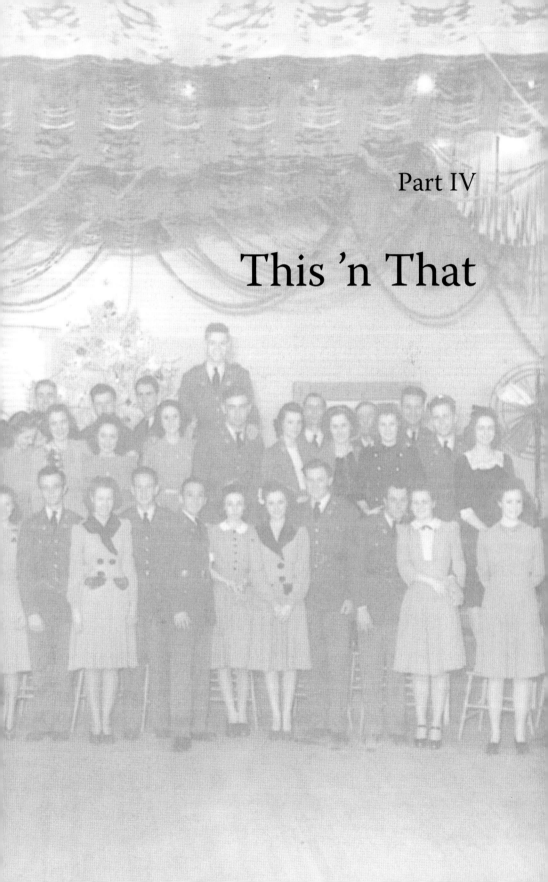

Part IV

This 'n That

Some Things Stay the Same, Others Change at Bonaventure Cemetery

It had been a while since I had driven through Bonaventure Cemetery, but with Christmas approaching, I thought it would be nice to pay a holiday visit to the place I remembered from childhood visits with my aunts.

Cemetery Director Jerry Flemming says visitors are still interested in finding the graves of many of Savannah's notables, including singer Johnny Mercer and poet Conrad Aiken. The grave of little Gracie Watson, however, is what most people ask about.

Gracie was six when she died in 1889. Her grave is marked by a life-sized statue sculpted by artist John Walz, who is also buried at Bonaventure. These days an iron fence surrounds Gracie's grave to preserve the delicate marble statue that so many people like to look at.

Visitors also ask about the Bird Girl statue made famous by the late Jack Leigh, who photographed it for the cover of John Berendt's bestseller about Savannah, *Midnight in the Garden of Good and Evil*. With all the hoopla surrounding the book, the statue was moved by the family and later exhibited at the Telfair Academy of Arts & Sciences, where it is today.

Jerry also said misinformed people come looking for the grave of Jim Williams, who actually is buried in a cemetery near his hometown of Gordon.

Jerry has high praise for the Bonaventure Historical Society, whose volunteers man the visitors' center on weekends. Members are continuing the legacy begun by the late Terry Shaw, whose dedication to Bonaventure was immeasurable.

"There is no one person who could replace Terry," Jerry said. Now, he added, several members are doing historical research, compiling the newsletter and completing other tasks that Terry undertook with joy for so many years. A brochure put together by the Historical Society has been extremely helpful to the cemetery staff and visitors alike.

I noticed when I drove through the gate that a sign posted at the entrance warns visitors not to leave valuables in their cars. Unfortunately, people tending graves or attending funerals have been victims of smash-

Visitors to Bonaventure Cemetery often ride by the statue of Gracie Watson. *Courtesy of the Savannah Morning News.*

and-grab thieves who shatter car windows and steal purses and other valuables left behind.

"It's sad that you have to remind people, but [thefts] can happen anywhere, even at the cemetery," Jerry said.

Even today, people believe that Bonaventure is "sold out" and that grave spaces are unavailable. Not true, said Jerry. Six-space lots in section T sell for $3,790.

So just when you thought that Bonaventure Cemetery was old news, there are a few new items to report.

First published in 2004 in the Morning News.

Guyton Gals Still Gathering

As girls growing up in Guyton, Thetis Carpenter Brinson and her pals would spend leisurely days walking the railroad tracks picking violets. "It was the greatest place because it was home," she said. "Guyton was the best spot on earth."

Thetis, who is "eighty-one going on eighty-two," and five of her childhood friends have met once a year since the 1940s. Thetis and Josephine Clarke Fahey graduated in 1942 from Guyton High School and the others "are about the same age," Thetis said. Although the gals now live hither and yon, they usually get together at different spots yearly during St. Patrick's Day week.

This year they met for lunch under the stars in the dining room at Johnny Harris's Restaurant. Thetis drove in from Sylvania, Josephine arrived from Tennessee, Mary Ida Carpenter Phillips popped in from Soperton, Martha Hodges Deason came from Macon, Evelyn Hodges Cook rode from Garden City and Louise Gilliam Zittrouer drove forty-five minutes or so from Guyton.

They greeted each other with hugs and smiles, and talked a bit about their memories of Guyton.

"Josephine and I were best friends before school, during school and after school," explained Thetis, who worked as a bookkeeper for the *Morning News* from 1942 until 1952. She then moved to Screven County because she met and married a "country boy," R. Edward Brinson. "He was a boy then but he's an old man now," Thetis teased.

The girls make time for each other because they want to catch up and find out what's going on in each other's lives, Thetis explained. "There aren't too many people who stay in touch with their childhood friends."

After she graduated from high school Josephine went to work for the Central of Georgia Railroad in Savannah and met her future father-in-law. "I didn't know he had a good-looking son," she said.

Evelyn, who turns eighty-five this month, says the great thing about Guyton was "knowing everybody." "You cared about everybody," she added.

The 1945 Christmas party at the *Savannah Morning News*. *From left*: Jack Cubbedge, Effie Suber, Rose Ackerman, Thetis Carpenter, Shirley Kramer and Valeria Barnes. Looking on at right with a cigar in his mouth is Herschel V. Jenkins. *Courtesy of Thetis Carpenter Brinson.*

Louise remembers the windowless calaboose, or jail, that once was a part of Guyton. Thinking about those convicts in a building without windows worried her, she said. In the small world department, Thetis and her family lived in an apartment in my late grandmother's house on Church Street and Louise took piano lessons from my late aunt, Lila Powers.

"I was the worst student Miss Lila ever had," she recalled. "She'd get aggravated with me and would let me go shopping for her." Louise later opened her own ballet, tap and jazz dancing school in Springfield.

Evelyn said when the girls were teenagers, the late Willie Grier Todd, who died recently, would "get a bunch of us together and teach us to dance and then we'd pull taffy." Others recalled jumping out of a barn window into a pile of hay and riding the spinning jenny.

Mary Ida attended the Methodist church in Guyton and has served as choir director at Soperton United Methodist Church for fifty-three years. "Guyton was a wonderful place to grow up," she said, echoing her longtime friends.

Louise was born in South Carolina but moved to Guyton as a child because her father ran the electric company. In those days, the lights would be turned off at a certain time. One night Louise "got caught" in the dark coming home and was terrified.

The Guyton gals say they'll keep getting together as long as they can drive or have someone drive them. Good friends gathering year after year to share precious memories: it's something we all should do.

First published in 2006 in the Morning News.

Library, Bookmobile Hold
Many Memories for This Rincon Native

Barbara Radford Jones grew up in Rincon but, as a child, was introduced to Savannah's public library via the bookmobile.

"The bookmobile stopped by our house once a month," she said. "My Grandpa, who lived next door to us, pushed his wheelbarrow out to the road each time to meet [the bookmobile] and pushed it back weighted down with his month's supply of reading. Grandpa read thirty to forty books each month and once had his picture along with his book-filled wheelbarrow in the local paper."

While growing up, Barbara said she was "thrilled" when her mother (Mary Nell Radford) was hired as a library clerk.

"Her position there opened up a whole new world for me," she wrote. "As a small child, just walking up the huge, stone steps and stepping into that enormous building was somehow magical. The tall ceilings and rows and rows of books awakened dreams and ideas inside my soul that I never knew were there. The library became a treasure box that my mother took us to time and time again.

"There were talented storytellers arranged by May McCall, director of the children's department...The first puppet show I ever saw, only one of many, was enjoyed in the children's department."

Back home in Rincon, Barbara wrote, "books became the dessert of our lives.

"Courage, adventure, friendships and compassion filtered down through the pages and onto our hearts as Mama read to us...Her words, her love of books and of us intertwined and wrapped itself around us. We were taught, not through words or lectures, reading models or educational programs, but through intimate moments sitting next to our Mama on the living room couch as she read that day's offerings to us...For this one small child and her little brother, the library books expanded our world and changed our perceptions about ourselves and others. Books brought light and joy into our ordinary daily lives. Thus we were blessed, for we learned early that books held the key to a life well lived."

Because of her mother's job at the library, Barbara and her brother were introduced to many special library employees, she said.

"Geraldine LeMay, head of the library, and her secretary, Mrs. Pottinger, were especially kind to us," she said. "We enjoyed the French accent, the first we had ever heard, of Miss Mauduit. As I grew up and began making reports for school, Margaret Godley in the reference department became a valuable ally. Frances Reese, director of the Chatham-Effingham Regional Library, treated us like family after my Mama had a terrible car accident on Highway 21 on her way to work one morning. Mama was in recovery for weeks at Memorial Hospital. Miss Reese invited me, by then a teenager, to stay with her in Savannah rather than make the twenty-mile drive back and forth to Rincon every night."

Barbara recalls that the "best gift" from the library did not come from a book but from a hand-written notice thumbtacked to the library's bulletin board.

The notice was for a room for rent to college students. Coincidentally, Barbara had just been accepted to Armstrong State College. With memories of her mother's accident still strong, she decided that she would stay in Savannah during the week and go home to Rincon on the weekends.

"Miss Reese knew the lovely lady who had posted the ad and who lived with her husband in a beautiful Cape Cod house on 57th Street just off Paulsen Street," she recalled. "The couple's children—two sons and a daughter—had all moved out to either get married or go off to universities elsewhere, and had left plenty of empty space…Occasionally, the oldest son and I crossed paths in his parent's home. I have now been married to that oldest son for over thirty years. Our careers brought us to Atlanta, but we will both retire in a few years to Savannah to the house on 57th.

"It's nice to know the library is still there with treasures, both bound and unbound, awaiting all who climb her steps and enter those doors. I wonder if I could sneak into a puppet show."

First published in the 2004 in the Morning News.

Jenkins Boys' Club Has Rich History

S.T. "Sam" McTeer is convinced that the athletic club started in 1933 by the late Judge Victor "Vic" Jenkins was a major factor in keeping many boys off the street and out of trouble during the Depression.

Vic, as he preferred to be called, was considered a mentor to hundreds of boys who grew up in Savannah in the 1930s, '40s and '50s. Even today the club he established in 1933 keeps boys busy with a wide array of sports. Most importantly, Sam said, Vic Jenkins was a role model and "teacher for all of us." Although the judge died in 1962, he isn't forgotten by the boys who gather at the Waters Avenue club that bears his name.

Each year on his birthday several boys hop aboard a tour bus and ride to Bonaventure Cemetery to place a wreath on the judge's grave. They also might participate in a quick quiz about the man who started the club. Questions might include: "Where is his portrait?" or "Where was he born?" (Not a bad idea for any school or organization named for a person.)

Sam and a group that includes Hal Griner, Sonny Smith and club director Billy Covington are planning a get-together for former club members. The event is still in the early stages, which means no date is set, but one will be announced as soon as plans gel. Currently, the reunion team is trying its best to locate former members.

Hal joined in 1946 and, like Sam, believes the Boys' Club was a positive influence on those who came before and after him. "For years," he said, "no boy who went through the club got into trouble…kids respected and obeyed [Vic] and if you didn't [follow the rules] you got kicked out."

For one thing, added Sonny, Vic wouldn't have stood for hooliganism. "He was the boss," Smith recalled. "He let the boys run the club but he was the boss."

All agreed that the judge devoted his entire adult life to the Boys' Club.

A lifelong bachelor, Vic Jenkins was born in Guyton in 1905. He attended Harvard Law School and began practicing law in Savannah. In the early

1930s he realized "a great need arose for organized and supervised activities for boys," according to a plaque inside the Boys' Club.

The club's first home was a garage on Jefferson Street. A year after the club was organized the Exchange Club of Savannah began sponsoring the Jefferson Athletic Club, as it was known then. Among the charter members were Harold Myers, Buck Stevens, Mack Chandler and others.

As the club grew, new quarters were needed, so the judge found a building on Henry Street between Bull and Drayton Streets. In 1945 the club began occupying quarters inside Odd Fellows Hall at State and Barnard Streets.

By 1948 the club had moved to Lincoln Street at 38th Street. One interesting note in that building's history is that songwriter Johnny Mercer donated $14,000 to the club in his father's honor to pay off the loan to build the Lincoln Street gym. In 1950 the Exchange Club began bringing the Coastal Empire Fair to Savannah to support the Boys' Club.

The club was on Lincoln until 1984, when a building was constructed at 6408 Waters Avenue. For many of those years—beginning in 1962—the late Sy Wright was director of the Boys' Club. Today that position is held by Billy Covington.

Vic left his entire estate to the Boys' Club and in 1963 the organization was renamed the Victor B. Jenkins Memorial Boys' Club.

First published in 2005 in the Morning News.

Jane Guthman Kahn's Scrapbook Is a Trip Down Memory Lane

When I was a child, our house had a screen door smartly decorated with a swirly kind of ironwork. A metal seagull, with wings outstretched, was smack dab in the middle. That door is long gone, but ever since I spotted it in the home movies, I have been enamored of those 1950s-era screen doors. I've even spotted a few on houses around town.

Longtime Savannahian Jane Guthman Kahn doesn't have a screen door, but she does have a fabulous scrapbook that chronicles not only her childhood days but news of the world as well. Jane, sixty-five, seems to be a kindred spirit. There are yellowed newspaper clippings, piano and dance recital programs, Girl Scout news, Broadway playbills, synagogue newsletters, politician and celebrity autographs, report cards, darling poems, photos and birthday cards.

"I imagine someone gave me the scrapbook," she said of the brown leather-like volume with a ship on the cover. She's not really sure what to do with these childhood memories. "I don't want to [tear it apart] and I don't think my children are interested."

A typed note from her grandfather, Abe Guckenheimer, reads: "This is not a letter, but simply a first-day mailing of the new stamp to be first put on sale at Savannah on May 22, 1944. Love and kisses from your grandfather."

An enclosed notebook offers this explanation: "These are poems by Guthman and [Alfred] Uhry. When they are read they cause a fury. Find the good ones, there are but a few. If you don't like them, I don't blame you." (Alfred Uhry, who is Jane's cousin, wrote *Driving Miss Daisy*.)

Alfred wrote about "The Cobbler": "The cobbler's name is Mr. Jones, He always buys us ice cream cones. He's very big, and round and fat, But we all love him that is that."

Various clippings pasted in the book are personal and newsworthy. One from the 1936 *Evening Press* has this headline: "Third Birthday...Little Miss Guthman Entertains With Party." Guests included Joan Byck, Nancy Solomon, Jane Sutcliffe, Barbara Smith, Richard Morrison, Charles

In the 1940s, Girl Scouts were able to visit the Liberty ship named for Juliette Low, the founder of the organization. *Courtesy of the Juliette Gordon Low Birthplace.*

Collatt, Harriet Schleuning, Charles Averitt, Mary Cunningham, Stephen Slenker, Melvin Adler Jr., Lee Kuhr, Mary Jane Maier, Edwin Feiler and Peggy Davis.

Others tell of the christening of the Liberty ship the S.S. *Juliette Low* and the death of Mayor Thomas Gamble. Absolutely no memory book would be complete without a pressed flower. Jane's is from a 1947 Girl Scout dance. "The first dance I ever enjoyed…" she wrote.

Apparently, Jane went through an autograph-collecting phase. There are signatures from Governor Eugene Talmadge, Senators Walter George and Richard Russell and pianist Arthur Rubinstein (along with a program from his 1947 concert at the Municipal Auditorium). Jane also secured the autograph of someone named Professor Quiz, along with this notation: "When Professor Quiz was here Betty Lord and I went. October, 1946." One of the most endearing requests comes from a letter Jane wrote to her cousin, Dr. Hans Schindler, who had a famous patient. On stationery engraved with "Jabber From Jane," she writes: "I read in the newspaper that Mr. Kreisler was your patient and I wondered if when he is better you could get his autograph for me. I am very much interested in him as I take piano lessons and I play his 'Viennese Melody.' I trust that Mr. Kreisler is progressing satisfactorily and that you and your family are well." This response came five days later, with her original letter enclosed (autographed by Mr. Kreisler): "I have your kind letter which really was a great surprise for me since I didn't know that I have such a nice and intelligent cousin…It gives me great pleasure to let you know that I was successful in obtaining an autograph from Mr. Kreisler."

Jane's poetry continued with this selection under a dog-eared 1945 news clipping: "The war is over, we hope for good. Through many tough battles we have stood. Peace is here, how glad we are…the war is over hurrah, hurrah."

I love strolling down memory lane (in my mind's eye it's an avenue decorated with 1950s-era screen door ironwork).

First published in 1999 in the Morning News.

Trip to Junk Store Yields
Sentimental Find

While in Atlanta recently I found a postcard of the old Tybee Hotel—a view that I had never seen before. I brought it home and stashed it in a bag with my other vintage postcards and made a mental note to come up with an ingenious way to display my collection.

Locally, I routinely stop by various shops to see what treasures await. A month or so ago, I found two wonderful books: *Brenda Starr, Girl Reporter* and *Polly of Pebbly Pit*, which will go on the mantel with my other Polly books.

Just last week I was driving by one of my haunts when I spotted a sign that said "new stuff." I took the bait, turned around, pulled into the parking lot and ventured in. I recognized some of the old stuff, but also noticed a thick black scrapbook on a lower shelf. I hauled it to a nearby tabletop and couldn't believe what I had found.

As an aside, I feel a bit uncomfortable when I see vintage family photographs in antique and junk stores. Yes, I usually look through them, but I often grow downhearted when I think how the smiling images were once part of someone's family. Somehow they ended up in a dusty box in a store where people like me paw through them.

It's a dirty job, but someone has to do it.

I opened the scrapbook and found photos, letters, telegrams and tons of other tidbits of someone's life. Among them were a picture of an Ardsley Park home, church choir snapshots, a sixth-grade photo from Charles Ellis School (June 1946) and a piano recital program listing my cousin, Mary Cargill Waddell, playing a tune called "Happy Valley."

I told the proprietor that I was stunned that this book of memories ended up in a store. He said that seeing such personal items used to bother him but it happens. When households are broken up sometimes only distant relatives or a trustee remain to pick up the pieces.

I turned the pages and read detailed captions below the photos: "This picture was taken at Nancy Cordray's house at White Bluff. We were out on the dock." (Nancy Cordray Barnwell was my first-grade teacher.)

The St. John's Boys' Choir was open to members of other churches. *Courtesy of the author.*

For a moment, I pictured my home office and the piles of "treasures" that are pleading to be organized. What's one more item? I thought a mere second before I heard myself saying, "So how much do you want for this?"

It was a done deal. I loaded someone else's memories into my car and headed home.

After this column ran with a picture of the St. John's Boys' Choir, I heard from Elliott Simmons, who sang with the group. He said he didn't know when he joined but was "pleasantly surprised" when the monthly payday came. "Mr. [Brooke] Reeve was in charge of this event during which he brought a cloth bag with a drawstring and spread the coins on the piano bench. As I recall, there were four rehearsals. We were expected to make at least three plus a tune-up before service on Sunday morning. Starting pay was twenty-five cents per month. That's right—twenty-five cents. Top pay was reserved for the boy soloists—Bobby Sullivan and Fred Stegin. As I recall they received five dollars each per month," said Simmons.

First published in 2004 in the Morning News.

Central of Georgia "Girls" Still Meet After All These Years

Some are pushing eighty but they still refer to themselves as the Central "girls," women who, decades ago, worked at the Savannah offices of the Central of Georgia Railroad. At least one of the gals was a nurse at the old Central Hospital on Bull Street at Washington Avenue, now headquarters for Senior Citizens Inc.

On the third Wednesday of every other month, they eat a leisurely meal, catch up on news and sometimes pass around old photos, like the tiny black-and-white snapshots Betty Hagan brought to their latest lunch.

"Look at Carolyn, how dark her hair was," said Betty, pointing to a young woman with shoulder-length, wavy hair.

The picture was probably taken during the 1940s when the railroad was bustling. They were posing in front of what the girls refer to as the "gray building" on what was then West Broad Street. The building at Hull Street is now part of the Savannah College of Art and Design.

As the pictures were inspected, some of the girls adjusted their bifocals to get a better look. One asked who in the photo was sharing the candy stick.

"Oh, that's Juanita," offered another as if it were yesterday. To most of these women, those days at the Central were happy ones because they made lifelong chums.

The group started with a half dozen making plans for lunch in 1954. One of those pioneers was Leila McClelland Bravo, who worked as a clerk in the passenger bureau.

"I counted all those tickets," she recalled. She was there nine years but quit in 1951, just before the birth of her first child.

Elizabeth Warner Butler Ress, who was attending her first Central lunch last month, worked in the accounting department in the railroad's red building.

Others at lunch, besides Elizabeth, Betty and Leila, included Theresa McClelland Richards, Betty Gnann, Catharine Fitzpatrick Kelly, Christine Aisendorf Rountree, Peggy Davis Galletta, Edna Cope Dooley, Sonia Heidt

Siebert, Milly Wolfe, Marguerite Salter, Ann Davis, Sara Martin Black, Margaret Dooley Lyons, Virginia Smith Nettles, Juanita Ward Lamb, Betty Cobb, Sheila Pierce Cobb and Pat Spencer Carlton.

Theresa Richards remembers that fateful day in 1963 when many of the women lost their jobs. It was June 19, to be exact, when a bulletin was posted that said: "As of 2 o'clock the following jobs will be abolished."

The glory days of the railroad had come to a screeching halt. Nevertheless, the working girls still made time for lunch and, nearly forty years later, continue to do so.

The women have no set program. They talk among themselves about a variety of subjects. Leila, who lives on the water, told her immediate lunch neighbors how her husband caught a 3½-pound trout in their crab trap. "I stuffed it with crab and we had it on Father's Day," she said proudly.

A few seats down a woman remembered how she came to Savannah during the Korean War as a young bride. They moved away but she returned after her husband died because she had made so many friends here.

"Many of us met our husbands [at the railroad]," another chimed in. Apparently it was love at first sight for Leila's future husband. He walked into the office, spotted her and asked a friend who she was. He told his buddy that she was the woman he was going to marry.

The railroad also was responsible for linking Sara Black with her husband, Lloyd. Sara worked with Lloyd's sister, Ann Davis, who introduced the pair.

First published in 2001 in the Morning News.

Still-Thriving Gordonston Garden Club Planted Roots Years Ago

Surrounded by a canopy of approximately five hundred pecan, magnolia and dogwood trees, a handful of neighbors decided to establish the Gordonston Garden Club.

It's a club rich in history and, this year, is celebrating its seventy-fifth anniversary. Members say the group will continue seasonal plantings and upkeep of the Gordonston entrance marker, plantings and Christmas decorations around the Gordonston Park gates and involvement in civic affairs related to history and the landscaped environment.

The club had its beginnings on a chilly day in January 1928 when Mrs. Herbert Salsbury invited fourteen friends to exchange gardening ideas. The meetings were held monthly in members' homes in Gordonston, which was originally the W.W. Gordon family farm.

That's Gordon, as in Juliette Gordon Low. No doubt, the feisty founder of the Girl Scouts would be charmed with what has become of the family farm and the accomplishments of the Gordonston Garden Club.

W.W. Gordon was Juliette's father. A section of land in Gordonston—which is a virtual oasis of trees and shrubs just east of Skidaway Road at Henry Street—was given to each of the Gordon children by their father. The portion given to Juliette is the site of a park that now bears her name.

Juliette forged the gates herself by hiring a blacksmith, taking lessons and making her own tools. With these, she beat copper into the shape of daisies, the flower, of course, being her nickname. The cornerstone for the gates was laid July 20, 1926, and the park was dedicated by the Gordon children in memory of their parents.

In the cornerstone Juliette placed the tools she had used to make the gates. (The tools and gates were later moved to the Juliette Gordon Low Birthplace.) In the 1940s, a rustic cottage was built in the park by Union

Bag and Paper Corp. and named the Calder Hut. It was to be used by the Girl Scouts, the Gordonston Association and the Garden Club.

Oftentimes the area, which is surrounded by an iron fence, is known as Brownie Park.

First published in 2003 in the Morning News.

"Tigers" Remember 1964 Journey to New York

Steve Hester was eleven in 1964 when his parents signed him up for a fabulous summer adventure: a seven-day bus trip to Virginia, Washington, Philadelphia and New York, including a visit to the 1964 World's Fair. He borrowed his sister's Brownie camera and boarded a Greyhound bus with thirty-five other Savannah-area boys.

The group, led by Tiger Athletic Club Director Fred Garis Jr., was for boys ages nine to fourteen who either played Tiger sports or worked for Mr. Garis at the club on Bee Road or at his camp at Tybee, Steve said. Approximate cost of the trip was $110 each. Mr. Garis advised the boys to pay for the trip by "asking for cash instead of Christmas presents...cutting grass and raking leaves."

What to take? In a handout, Mr. Garis listed, "Comics, camera and film, one suitcase large enough for all belongings...extra pair comfortable shoes...Bermuda shorts...and $15 spending money, which will be given out equally each day."

The trip was a "great adventure" for a boy who was going "seriously away from home" for the first time, Steve recalled. "Of course, I felt safe with Mr. Garis and the other [chaperones]," who included William Goolsby and Chuck Davis.

Brothers Curtis and Walter Lewis remember watching the New York Mets play the San Francisco Giants at Shea Stadium. "It was my one and only time at Shea Stadium," Curtis said. The highlight of that game, Walter said, was seeing Willie Mays hit a home run.

Before they arrived in New York, the group made several stops in Virginia, including Luray Caverns and Williamsburg. With his sister's Brownie safely around his neck, Steve snapped several pictures inside Luray Caverns, not realizing that they wouldn't come out.

Steve said his mother packed a grocery bag full of snacks for the trip, which "half the [boys on the] bus" enjoyed. "We all had a big time," he said.

Swimming in motel pools was a thrill, Steve added. "I vividly remember swimming relays against Tommy Bond. Of course, I had Bluffton training behind me," he said confidently, referring to Bluffton, South Carolina, where many Savannahians own second homes.

Fred Garis Jr., who started the Tiger Club, also offered classes at Stubbs Hardware. *Courtesy of the Fred Garis Jr. family.*

Unfortunately, Steve left his favorite bathing suit hanging out to dry at one of the motels. The suit may have been forgotten at the Roses of Picardy Motel in Colonial Heights, Virginia, where a souvenir Confederate $1 million bill advises holders to "save this, the South shall rise again."

The big city of New York City proved to be an eye-opening experience for the boys. "I remember riding the subway a time or two," Curtis said, adding that the group stayed in a hotel in Times Square.

Steve recalled how he and others were tossing water balloons from the hotel windows and having the bellmen fuss at them. He also remembers riding the subway and not understanding why a mother holding a baby was standing while the men were sitting.

When he asked Mr. Garis why they wouldn't be gentlemen and offer her their seats, Mr. Garis said, "Son, that's just the way it is in New York."

Steve also was shocked to see that ice cream, which cost maybe $0.25 in Savannah, was $1.25 in New York. The city's size, price differences and the social environment were something new for most of the boys. He said he "can hardly remember Washington," but he does recall going up to the top of the Washington Monument and "taking my Brownie shots."

Other boys who were scheduled to go on the trip, according to Mr. Garis's roster, were Sherrod Patterson, David Jelks, Thomas Scardino, Billy Winburn, Carl Roebling, Alan Williams, Bruce Ladson of Vidalia, Billy

Bond, Howard Smith, Tony Fine, Olin McIntosh, Frank Durkin, Harry King, Matt Barfield, Cregg Propst, Ricky Timms, Will Burgstiner, Bill and Kirk Campbell of Brunswick, Matt Sanders, Tim Harriott, Howard Reeve, Ricky and Bobby Buechner, Billy Mordecai, Millard Long, Mark Smith, Gene Brogdon, Lloyd and Edward Brown and Thomas and Campbell Cox of Darlington, South Carolina.

First published in 2004 in the Morning News.

Sometimes It's Hard To Say So Long to a Beloved Building

Today Abercorn Street just south of DeRenne Avenue is a virtual racetrack, bustling with retail businesses, motels, restaurants, doctors' offices and everything in between.

But tucked between a video store and a pawnshop is an oasis of sorts: a sparkling white building with its sweeping front lawn and drive that resembles a Southern plantation house.

The former Sipple's Mortuary—most recently Gamble Funeral Home—has been a landmark on that stretch of Abercorn for decades. In a few days, however, the grand old building will be no more. Construction begins soon on a retail center that will include Fresh Market and other upscale stores.

For Charlie Sipple, whose family constructed the building in 1960, the demolition has prompted mixed emotions. "It's good and bad," he said.

On one hand it's good to have such high-end stores come into the community. On the other, the building has sentimental value. But, as Charlie pointed out, "You just have to swing with the times."

He had similar thoughts in 1955 when he returned to Savannah from the Air Force. Sipple and other family members knew it was time to move the family funeral home from its downtown location at Bull and Jones Streets. Parking was only one of many concerns. "We couldn't renovate," he recalled. "We knew we had to build from the ground up."

Charlie had a talk with his father, who finally agreed to a new location. They heard about a tract of land off White Bluff Road that had once been home to a place called the Gold Star Ranch.

"I remember as a little boy on Sundays after church my parents taking me out there," he said. "They had a Ferris wheel, a merry-go-round and all kinds of rides."

Charlie, along with his sister and her husband, Ralph Kuhn, persuaded Charlie's father to purchase roughly five acres for the new home of Sipple's.

Relocating the business to what was then the edge of town was a progressive move, considering that Abercorn came to a screeching halt at DeRenne back then.

"I could barely comprehend the projected commercialization of that area," Charlie said. "There were no malls then or anything, but [planners] said Abercorn would eventually go out to [Interstate 95]."

The building, which resembled something out of *Gone With the Wind*, was built by the Artley Co. Charlie credits his mother, Nora, with coming up with the building's facade.

It opened in 1960. By that time Abercorn reached as far as Stephenson Avenue.

Charlie's father, Charles Sipple Jr., was a dentist, but suffered a serious heart attack two weeks after Charlie was born and couldn't continue practicing. "My parents bought the funeral home from my father's brothers and sisters," he said.

The Sipple family operated the mortuary until the late 1980s, when they sold the business and equipment to a national chain, but they held on to the property. All the while, Charlie worked part-time at the funeral home with folks such as Ed Gamble, who in recent years ran a funeral home on the site.

Now Ed is building his own funeral home on Stephenson Avenue. Charlie will continue his association with Ed when the new building opens early next year.

Sometimes it's just hard to say goodbye to things—and buildings—that are loved.

First published in 2004 in the Morning News.

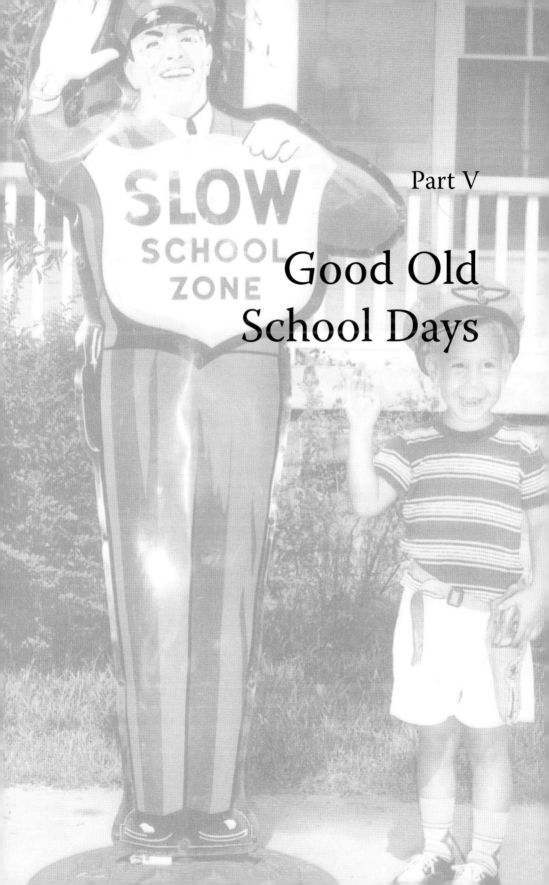

Part V

Good Old
School Days

St. Michael's School Celebrates Milestone

It was the late 1940s on sleepy little Tybee Island. Two-laned Butler Avenue still had palm trees running down its middle and a Catholic grade school called St. Michael's opened its door. A handful of Franciscan nuns were dispatched from Boston to teach on the island and the Ellzeys, Chus and other Tybee families enrolled their children at the new school.

Patti Barnwell Red entered the fifth grade at St. Michael's in 1948 when her family moved from Savannah to the beach. Catholic schools were nothing new to Patti—she had attended Sacred Heart in Savannah—but a kickball-playing nun at St. Michael's was, indeed, something else.

The athletic nun had to "pull up her [floor-length] habit a little bit to run," Patti recalled. "That was the first time that I realized that nuns had ankles."

That monumental moment is one of dozens of memories Patti chatted about this week as she prepared for the fiftieth anniversary celebration at St. Michael's. The school is on Lovell Avenue at its intersection with Eighth Street, which was a half-block away from the Barnwell home.

"Whenever one of the nuns needed something, they'd call us," Patti recalled. "In the winter, when it got so cold in the church, we would have Mass in one of the classrooms. My sister and I would have to carry the portable kneelers from the church to the school." If the nuns requested your help, there was no beating around the bush, Patti said. "You went."

Patti was salutatorian in 1952 and one of only five students in St. Michael's first graduating class. The other graduates were Patricia Mann (Janisheck), Hubert Ellzey Jr., Lester Hiers (Wright) and Mola Chu (Jung). "Hubert deserved a medal for being the only boy in our class," she said, laughing.

Statuesque Patti also remembers being crowned May Queen and "feeling like an Amazon. I hated it."

The "mostly Irish" nuns who taught Patti and her St. Michael's pals were the "dearest, sweetest, most charitable nuns in the world," she said.

Certain lay people involved with the school, especially those who were kind to children, made an impression on Patti.

Lizzie Farrell was one she can't forget. "Miss Lizzie set the style for everyone on the island," she recalled. "Every Christmas the Volunteer Fire Department would bring Santa Claus to the school and throw a party for the children. I remember one year looking up at Santa Claus. Do you know who it was? It was Miss Lizzie."

Another unforgettable character was Catherine Roach, who played the organ at St. Michael's if a nun wasn't available.

"She stands out in my mind as being so patient with us—we definitely were kids who couldn't sing," Patti confessed. Mildred Burke was another kind soul who was always ready to help with any church or school function, no matter what.

Patti's younger sisters and brothers, as well as her two daughters, all attended St. Michael's and she holds the distinction of being the first graduate to have a child graduate from the school.

First published in 1998 in the Morning News.

BC "Survivors" Club Offers Lunch but No Dues or Speeches

Sam McTeer comes from the old school, literally. That's the affectionate term he uses to describe Benedictine Military School when it was at its original location at 34th and Bull Streets.

McTeer also is a member of a club that guarantees no dues, fees, speeches, officers, fundraising and "no duties whatsoever." This unique organization is the newly formed BC Survivors Club, a Dutch treat luncheon group for those who attended BC when it was the old school.

"The purpose is to enjoy fellowship with old, and I mean old, schoolmates," explained McTeer, who is a 1941 BC graduate.

Webster, meanwhile, defines old school as meaning "a group of people who cling to traditional or conservative ideas," which could possibly describe McTeer and buddies like Jack Stacy, David Kelly, Bert Trapani and Buddy Fischer who started the club.

The longtime Savannahians decided the guys from the old school would meet on the second Monday of the even months, that is February, April, June, October and December.

Originally, BC classes from 1938 to 1944 were invited. "That made it the three classes before and after us," McTeer explained. "We had to start somewhere."

"I went by the school and picked up the class lists," he added. He wrote a letter telling the guys that "we plan on meeting on a regular basis to enjoy a meal while we reminisce." McTeer continued: "I'm sure that each member will have some interesting and possibly humorous stories to tell, some fabricated, of course."

Thirty-five guys showed up at Johnny Harris's Restaurant for that first meeting.

Because of the grand turnout, it was decided that the classes 1945 and 1946 would be added to the mailing list with more classes included later, depending on the interest. Five additional BC graduates came to the June lunch, although McTeer insists that anyone who attended—not necessarily graduated from—the old school is eligible.

Stacy says he enjoys getting together and "telling lies" to his old buddies, some of whom went directly from their junior year at BC into the service during World War II. "Some of these guys never finished BC but that's OK," he said. "Anyone who attended the old school is welcome."

First published in 2002 in the Morning News.

Savannah Christian Cofounder Remembers School's Early Days

Harold Deane Akins is a determined woman. Her late husband, the Reverend George Akins, was equally persistent. So more than fifty years ago, the daring duo relied on strong faith and started the first Christian school in Savannah. Today that school is called Savannah Christian Preparatory School, one of the largest private educational institutions in the city.

"We were the pioneers," Mrs. Akins said. "The other day I came across some papers that George had written a long time ago. One was entitled 'The Purpose of Savannah Christian School.'"

The purpose was twofold, she said: to bring as many young people as possible to a saving knowledge of our Lord and Savior Jesus Christ; and to help them grow in grace and knowledge of Jesus Christ. The school's slogan was "Where the Bible comes first."

"My prayer is that the original purpose will never be forgotten," Mrs. Akins said.

The Akinses met at Toccoa Falls Bible College. Akins was a student and Mrs. Akins—who was then Harold Deane Thomason (she was named for her father)—was attending a summer camp. They married five years later.

"After George and I were married, we started having Bible clubs every weekday afternoon in different parts of [Savannah]," Mrs. Akins recalled. "These clubs led to a large Vacation Bible School at the Union Mission on Liberty Street. Then God laid the Mission Youth Camp on our hearts."

The camp opened in 1947 on property near what was then the end of Telfair Road. Opening a Christian school remained a priority for the Akinses. Money began trickling in as Akins described in his book, *Miracles in My Life*. Dr. and Mrs. Newell Turner gave Akins $2,500, which was the first monetary gift for the planned school. The final donation in a fundraising month dubbed the January Miracle came from Waldo Bradley.

The dream of a Christian school started to become a reality.

Children who attended school during the Cold War may remember practicing civil defense drills and walking to the railroad tracks. *Courtesy of the* Savannah Morning News.

Good Old School Days

In 1951, Anna Clarke was named the first principal and, upon her retirement, Mrs. Akins, who holds a master's degree in education, was named her successor. The Akinses retired in 1973 and left a legacy that remains today.

Afterward, Mrs. Akins taught at South College for seventeen years. Reverend Akins died in 1999 at age ninety-one.

First published in 2001 in the Morning News.

Former Savannah High School Building Has Rich History

In 1937, when Savannah High School was dedicated at 500 Washington Avenue, it was the largest high school in Georgia. A history of the school offers these bits of trivia: the distance around the perimeter of the building is just under a quarter of a mile and *Gone With the Wind* could have been written in its entirety on the 12,800 square feet of chalkboard.

From a student's viewpoint, Mary McPeters Price, who graduated in Savannah High's June 1938 class, the building was "gleaming and shiny."

"It was thrilling and wonderful that we could have such a school," she recalled. (Prior to the opening of the new school, Savannah High was at 208 Bull Street, where the school system's administrative offices are now.)

Getting to and from school "required some ingenuity" because most students were accustomed to walking, said Mrs. Price, whose family lived near Forsyth Park. "My sister taught at Romana Riley and had the car so she took me," she recalled.

Mrs. Price was especially excited when Principal John Varnedoe gave his permission for a girls' basketball team—the first ever at the school. "He said yes if we could find an advisor."

Teacher Mabel Bryant was recruited as advisor and the girls began practicing in the school gym, which had been missing from the school's downtown location.

Memorable teachers included Ellie Freedman and Lola Stevens, who led the Glee Club, which performed at the dedication.

Savannah High was built on the site of what was supposed to be a grand hotel that, literally, never got off the ground. When plans for the hotel went kaput, the Board of Education took over the property and built what was then "new" Savannah High with WPA funds. The cost of the project was approximately $900,000. An even newer SHS was built in the 1990s on Pennsylvania Avenue and the Washington Avenue building became the Savannah Arts Academy.

Good Old School Days

To many of those who attended the school at 500 Washington Avenue, the building will always be Savannah High, which is what a new historical marker says.

When the building was dedicated in 1937, the *Savannah Morning News* described the ceremony as "appropriate exercises which marked the long-sought culmination of a civic dream for adequate facilities for the education of boys and girls."

Before the school was moved to Washington Avenue, the powers that be considered changing the name to James E. Oglethorpe High School. Again the *Morning News* editors commented: "It would have been a grievous mistake to have given the new school the name of any individual. It is in every respect a Savannah institution and as such should bear the name of the city it is to serve so magnificently."

First published in 2002 in the Morning News.

Hancock School's Fiftieth Celebration Capped an Emotional Few Days

The first day of April 2002 started out like most at Hancock Day School. Parents pulled their cars into the drop-off line as staffers dutifully directed freshly scrubbed children to their classrooms.

Plans were in full swing for a busier-than-usual week. The school's annual Field Day was approaching and, two days after that, a grand reception—in the works for months—was to honor administrators Bill and Doris Bell on the occasion of the school's fiftieth anniversary.

But suddenly that morning, excitement turned to concern. At approximately 8:15 a.m. Bill Bell suffered a heart attack in the school office. A pair of ambulances, with sirens wailing, interrupted the orderly line of cars. Paramedics jumped out and raced up to the school gate to tend to the man everyone in Hancock circles refers to as Mr. Bell.

Those watching and those who quickly heard the bad news feared the worst. But after angioplasty and the placement of a stint, Mr. Bell soon was holding court in a room at Memoria Health University Center.

"We felt the prayers," Mrs. Bell recalled in a letter sent to Hancock parents. "They uplifted us and gave us hope. So many blessings flowed that April 1st."

The following Friday Mr. Bell was released from the hospital. On the way home, Mrs. Bell took a slight detour and drove by the field where Hancock children were participating in sack races, relays and the popular tug of war.

Even then parents and friends wondered if Mr. Bell would be strong enough to make it to the fiftieth anniversary of the school his late mother opened in 1953.

Concerned folks didn't need to worry. The following Sunday Mr. and Mrs. Bell greeted hundreds of former students and longtime friends at the "glorious" reception that Mrs. Bell described as "one of the best experiences we've ever had."

"We were so absolutely touched. It made our hearts feel so good," she added. "We felt so very, very blessed."

In the early days, Bill and Doris Bell attended Hancock School's graduation ceremonies with school founder Emmie Ruth Hancock, who was Bill's mother. *Courtesy of the* Savannah Morning News.

Mrs. Bell said seeing former students "made us proud and humble that we are doing what we are doing."

On that day, Mrs. Bell said she knew her late mother-in-law was smiling down from heaven. Seeing hundreds of friends, several of whom came from out of town, was "wonderful" and "utterly amazing," she added.

"Mr. Bell is doing much better and has more energy than he had before the angioplasty," his wife said. "We say our prayers, keep our fingers crossed and listen to our doctors."

No doubt, watching the children at school and sticking to his routine of policing the carpool lines is probably the best medicine for this educator who is revered by so many.

First published in 2003 in the Morning News.

Saying Goodbye but Not for Long

It was just about a year ago that stunned Hancock Day School parents received a letter from Bill and Doris Bell saying that Hancock was closing. Looking back, though, parents and others associated with the school had wondered how long the Bells, who have no children, would continue.

The couple, who had devoted their lives to educating thousands of children, admitted it was difficult to say goodbye but knew it was time they focus on their health.

Barely a week after the letter came out, a standing-room-only crowd of parents and teachers gathered at a nearby church to discuss plans to keep the school open. In only a few weeks' time, parents breathed a sigh of relief to hear that their beloved Hancock would remain open at the Skidaway Road location with the same faculty and staff.

The Bells already had agreed to sell the property to Southside Baptist Church, but the church allowed the school to lease the land for three years.

Now Hancock is actively looking for a new site. Headmistress Pat Crews, who is both a former teacher and parent of Hancock students, described the transition as smooth. Bill Bell stops by often but doesn't direct carpool anymore. Most other Hancock traditions, however, remain intact: the Harvest Festival, the Thanksgiving Feast and the fifth-graders' trip to Washington, D.C. The wooden "Mind Your Manners" sign is still posted for all students to see when they walk though the front gate.

The school is now operated by a twelve-member board of trustees made up of parents, grandparents, the Bells, Crews and veteran Hancock teacher Brenda Brown, who is wearing two hats: first-grade teacher and curriculum director. An open slot on the board has been set aside for a community leader.

Word of mouth has kept enrollment steady. When the Bells retired, the student population stood at 161. When the 2004–05 school year began, 147 students were enrolled in classes from pre-kindergarten to fifth grade.

One of the first questions posed to Crews by prospective parents is what will happen when the lease with the church runs out.

"I tell them that the future of Hancock is very bright," she said. "In three years Hancock Day School will still exist, but just not at 5526 Skidaway Road."

First published in 2005 in the Morning News.